Turning Points
in World History

GEOFFREY
BARRACLOUGH

Turning Points
in World History

THAMES AND HUDSON

For Charis
With Love and Gratitude

First published in Japan in 1977 by
Nippon Hoso Shuppan Kyokai

© Geoffrey Barraclough 1977
English language edition © Geoffrey Barraclough 1979

Library of Congress Catalog card number 79-63881
Printed and bound in Great Britain

Contents

Preface

This book originates in a television series broadcast in Japan in 1974 and published in Tokyo in 1977 under the title *Bunmei ni totte no henkaku-ki* (Turning Points in Civilization). The first four chapters are an English version of the broadcasts, occasionally updated and adapted for an English-speaking audience. The fifth chapter has been specially written for this edition. It derives from an exchange of views between myself and Professor Shozaburo Kimura which followed the lectures, and though none of the opinions expressed should be attributed to Professor Kimura, I should like to thank him warmly for raising a number of interesting questions and encouraging me to think again about some important issues. I am also grateful to the Japanese broadcasting corporation Nippon Hoso Kyokai for inviting me to deliver this course of lectures, and I am glad to have this opportunity of expressing my gratitude to my friend Stanley Baron, who not only suggested publishing the lectures in English but also undertook the onerous task of preparing the English text.

November 1978   G.B.

A world
through European eyes

1

Two great questions have confronted us all in the last twenty-five years – first, the great conflict which has divided the world, the conflict between communism and capitalism and between the United States and Soviet Russia, between the ideologies of socialism and liberalism. We may call it a struggle for the hearts and souls of men, a struggle which has drawn in peoples everywhere, peoples who really had no direct interest or part in it but who, in a global world such as we inhabit, could not isolate themselves from it. And second, the changing relationship between Europe and the rest of the world, 'the great dialogue', as Arnold Toynbee once called it, between the world and the West, the reaction of Asia and Africa to western domination, to the culture imposed by Europeans over most of the world's surface, most of the world's peoples, in a great all-engulfing movement which came to its peak in the seventy-five years between 1880 and 1955.

The first of these questions, the Cold War and its implications, the polarization of the world between the Soviet Union and the United States, between the socialist and the capitalist camps, I shall return to later. At present I want to discuss Europe's place in the world – Europe's role in world history.

At first glance the question seems very simple. The French scholar, Paul Valéry, called Europe a 'peninsula of Asia', a western appendix of the great Eurasian land mass. How was it that this western appendix came to be in a position to exercise this power, this domination over the greater part of the world? Clearly, in size, in population, it is far inferior to Asia. What gave Europe the strength it possessed at the end of the nineteenth century? The answer is its quite extraordinary technological and scientific proficiency, its machines, its weapons, and of course its shipping, which at that time was of the greatest importance. The great revolution in transport and communications during the last third of the nineteenth century, which came about with the supersession of sailing ships by steam power-driven ships and then by oil-driven ships, was the factor which made it possible for the Europeans to control the oceans and the sea-routes and to impose their hegemony on the rest of the world.

So much, I think, is obvious; but it tells us very little. Science and technology, after all, do not arise of themselves by a process of spontaneous generation. Why did the scientific and technological revolution take place in Europe and not elsewhere? Why not, for example, in China, which had once been scientifically far in advance of Europe? What were the peculiar qualities of European society, the special conditions which made the scientific and technological revolution possible? Why were Europeans rather than Africans or Japanese predisposed to scientific investigation and technological innovation?

Once we ask these questions, things are far less clear and a whole range of possibilities opens out. Europeans, perhaps characteristically, have sought the answer in the investigation of economic facts. Ever since the American economist Walt Rostow first used the term 'take-off', there has been a great deal of research into the causes of what is called 'take-off into sustained growth'. Rostow and others examined the economic preconditions of the Industrial Revolution, particularly the Industrial Revolution in Great Britain which they rightly saw as the seed-bed of the modern world, seeking in that way to establish the reasons for the causes of the take-off, and hoping also to discover how less developed or underdeveloped countries could take off into sustained growth.

It is unnecessary to discuss the arguments and controversies which followed; the upshot was that even economists and economic historians came to the conclusion that take-off cannot be explained in economic terms alone – for example, simply as a result of a high rate of capital accumulation – but rather that it must be related to the total situation in any given society. It must be related to the climate of ideas and to the social structure as they had developed over time.

So far as social structure is concerned, historical demography (it is a new study, scarcely more than twenty years old) has disclosed one significant difference between early modern Europe in the seventeenth and at the beginning of the eighteenth centuries and other pre-industrial societies. This difference helps to explain, at least in part, why Western Europe was able to escape the well known, constantly repeated cycle of population overtaking resources and giving rise to famines and epidemics – the cycle which in other pre-industrial societies habitually frustrated sustained economic growth and expansion. Historical demography has shown that in Western Europe, as contrasted for example with India, late marriage and family limitation preserved a relatively favourable ratio of resources to population. In Asia, as any reader of Gandhi's autobiography will know, a young couple (in his case, as in many others, very young) sets up house with the husband's parents. In Europe, marriage was normally postponed until the resources were available to set up an independent household, and the result of this was the creation of a pattern of saving and a propensity to save which encouraged capital accumulation and thus furthered economic growth. This has shed new light on the factors, or at least on some of the factors, which enabled Western Europeans to accumulate the economic and therewith the political power which ultimately underpinned their imperial expansion in the nineteenth century.

The reason why I have used this example is that it shows us that the question why Europe took off into modern industrial society far ahead of all other countries is fundamentally an historical one. We speak of historical demography, but in reality what we are dealing with is human attitudes, people's attitudes to their family, to their marriage, to reproduction. These attitudes cannot be explained simply in crude materialistic or economic terms; they are a question of human behaviour. The economic strength of nineteenth-century Europe and its technological efficiency are obvious enough; they are facts we can all see. But why that particular economic and technological development occurred in Europe and nowhere else can only be explained by studying European history.

We do not know (or at least I do not know) why the attitudes of Europeans to the family were different from the attitudes of Asians and Africans, why they imposed restraints on the size of the family, whereas among Africans, for example, a large family was commonly regarded as a boon, a blessing and a benefit. We do not know either (or at least I do not know) exactly when this change of attitude occurred. It certainly did not exist from the beginning of European history. It occurred at some specific point of time in the development of European society. That is why I call the problem an historical one. In other words, it is a question of the formation of specific attitudes in the course of historical development, and if there is anything distinctive about Europe – and of course there is – then it is something formed by and arising from its history.

If we want to know the place of Europe in the world, we must turn to its history; of course it must be the right sort of history, and not what Matthew Arnold called 'that great Mississippi of falsehood'. Too much history written by Europeans concentrates on Europe as though nothing else, nowhere else, really mattered; by the same token, the classical historians of China looked on the Middle Kingdom as the centre of the world. It is a commonplace that history as seen by Europeans was until very recently, and often still is, 'Eurocentric'. But we must not make too much of this. Every culture is considered to be unique and superior by the people who share it – partly, of course, because of ignorance of other cultures. What made 'Eurocentrism' different from and more dangerous than the ethnocentrism of other countries was the spread of European civilization throughout the world.

When the Chinese emperor, the Son of Heaven, told the British envoy at the end of the eighteenth century that England had nothing to offer China that it wanted, the English could afford to laugh at Chinese contempt. The Son of Heaven wrote to Queen Victoria as though she were a minor tributary, but he could not force her to pay tribute, as he did the Vietnamese, or the Koreans, or the Tibetans. His ethnocentrism was relatively harmless. But the ethnocentrism of Europeans was a different thing. Because their science and technology made them powerful, able to interfere with other peoples in Asia and Africa and South America, they convinced themselves that their values were universal values, that European philosophy, European jurisprudence, European political ideas – even European music and painting – were not only the best but were destined to prevail universally. So they constructed a view of world history to fit these assumptions. It is a view of world history which converges on Europe, in which civilization passes from people to people until it comes to rest in Europe and in the outlying Europe across the Atlantic, the United States of America. Not for nothing is the first introductory history course in nine out of ten American colleges and universities called 'An Outline of Western Civilization'. The assumption is that this is the civilization that matters, and that the task of the historian is to trace, stage by stage, its origins and growth, pointing out the contribution of Greece, the contribution of Rome, the contribution of Christianity, the contribution of the Renaissance, and so on.

This type of history, far from enabling us to assess Europe's place in world history, obscures and perverts it. As I wrote a number of years ago, a history that concentrates on the civilization of Western Europe may serve to fortify us in our belief in the superiority of our European traditions and values, but nothing is more likely to mislead and misinform us about the factors which determined the course of events at any particular time. We can only see what was unique about Europe – where it followed the same path as other civilizations and where it diverged – if we look at its history comparatively: in comparison with the history of China, or India, or Japan, or of the Islamic peoples of the Fertile Crescent, the bridgehead between the Iranian upland and the Nile valley and North Africa. Comparison will show us what was important and what was not; and a great deal that looms large in traditional accounts of European history will seem trivial and parochial if we look at it in a global perspective.

When we look at European history in a world perspective, the first result is that many of the conventional landmarks fade away. For Europeans the central theme of their history, as presented in scores of history books, is the rise of the nation states – France, England, Germany, and the rest – and their relations, the struggle between them for hegemony, first the attempt by Spain, then the attempt by France, finally the attempt by Germany, to impose its rule on Europe. European history is divided into periods by the names of the predominant statesmen: the age of Louis XIV, the age of Napoleon, the age of Bismarck. From the point of view of world history, this way of looking at the European past is far too narrow. When we call the years between 1870 and 1890 the 'age of Bismarck', we mean that Bismarck raised Germany to the front rank among the European powers, and was the dominant figure in European diplomacy. But front rank among the European powers was very different from front rank among the world powers. As an industrial power Germany was rapidly catching up with and overtaking Great Britain. Just as rapidly, it was being overtaken by the United States. In an age of imperialism, it could not compete with the British navy and the British merchant fleet. Limit your view to continental Europe, and Bismarck seems a dominating figure; extend it to the world, and he falls back into the second rank. What we call the 'age of Bismarck' is really, from a global point of view, the time when Europe was being dwarfed by the great extra-European powers, Russia (with one foot in Europe and the other in Asia) and the United States. It is the time when the European balance of power was being replaced by the world-wide intercontinental balance of power under which we live today. What mattered in a world perspective were the contacts between the expanding imperialisms of Great Britain, Russia and the United States on the north-west frontiers of India, in Persia, in China and in the islands of the Pacific. These contacts and the conflicts that arose from them are of fundamental importance because, unlike the international relations of Bismarck's Europe, they were the beginning of a new era in world history.

Or turn back to the thirteenth century. The main themes of European history in that century, as presented in the history books, are the rise and consolidation of the national monarchies in France, Spain and England, the development of English parliamentary institutions after Magna Carta in 1215, the beginnings of the long rivalry between England and France, which resulted in the Hundred Years War, and the conflict of empire and papacy, bringing about the collapse of Germany's position in Europe after the death of the Emperor Frederick II in 1250. If we widen our perspective and look at Europe in world history, the things that stand out are very different. The central fact of European history in the thirteenth century was, without any reasonable doubt, the Mongol onslaught, the appearance of the Mongols in the eastern borderlands of Europe, the great conquering sweep of the Mongol people under Genghis Khan and his son Ogdai Khan, which not only extended their sway to China and vast tracts of Asia but also carried them across the Russian steppes to Hungary, Poland and eastern Germany. From the point of view of world history, the focus of events in thirteenth-century Europe was in the east, not in the west, and this means that, instead of concentrating on the national monarchies in the west, we should pay far more attention to the eastern borderlands of Europe, particularly to Russia, which bore the brunt of the Mongol invasions.

What we see here is the ethnocentricity of historians in Western Europe, which has blinded them not only to what was going on in the world beyond Europe, but also to really decisive aspects of European history as well. Equally misleading is the way Europeans divide history into periods – the Dark Ages, the Middle Ages, the Renaissance, the Reformation, and so on. All periodizations of history, no doubt, are artificial to some extent; but they should, at least, be based on events of universal, not merely of local, importance. These are not.

The conventional starting points of modern history for European historians are the Renaissance and the Reformation. The reason for picking out these events is well known. They are regarded as a turning point because (so it is alleged) this was the time when the minds of Europeans were liberated from the control of the Church, when the human spirit was freed, at least in Europe, to explore nature, to explore man and the world, when the spirit of inquiry which was to be the mark of European civilization at last became a dominant characteristic. Once again I do not want to spend time criticizing this view in detail. No doubt it contains some elements of truth. But in two important ways it is unsatisfactory. The first is that this division of history – the division between medieval and modern history – is confined to Europe alone. No such break occurred elsewhere in the world at the turn of the fifteenth and the sixteenth centuries of the Christian era. In other words, it reflects a distinctly Eurocentric view of history. Secondly, it leaves some fundamental questions unanswered. Neither the Renaissance nor the Reformation was as distinctive an event as this interpretation suggests. There had been other renaissances in Europe before the fifteenth century, actually a whole series of renaissances reaching back to the ninth century, and there had been reformers without number long before Martin Luther – Wyclif in England, Huss in Bohemia, to name only the two most prominent. But the earlier reforms had withered and faded away. Why was it that the sixteenth century registered a permanent advance whereas other centuries had experienced only a temporary stimulus? What was the new factor which so changed the external environment that the decisive leap into the future, which had baffled earlier generations, suddenly become feasible?

The answer, of course, is the discovery of a new world and at the same time the voyages, explorations, journeys of discovery which were carried out from Europe through the Atlantic around Africa into the Indian Ocean, and from there through the strait of Malacca into the China Seas. At the end of the fifteenth century Europe was only one of half a dozen great civilizations – the Chinese civilization, the Indian civilization, the Islamic civilization which at this time was at the beginning of a great resurgence under the Safavids of Persia and the Ottoman Turks, and in Africa the empire of Songhai with its astounding wealth in gold. These civilizations all had their own separate existence. Only in the cold, snow-bound northern regions of Eurasia were there still nomadic peoples. But of these great civilizations Europe was only one, and certainly at the end of the fifteenth century by no means the most important, the most civilized, or the most wealthy. Yet by the end of the eighteenth century the situation had changed completely. Europe had gained control of the ocean routes and organized an immensely profitable world-wide commerce, and had also conquered vast territories in the Americas, in India and in Siberia. In the perspective of world history this period stands out then as a period of transition from the isolated regions of earlier centuries, when Europe, China, Japan, India, etc., were all going their own ways, to the integrated 'one world' of the nineteenth century, and in the same perspective we can see how the place of Europe in the world has also changed.

Down to 1492, when Columbus discovered America, European society, for all its political upheavals, had been basically a static society. Apart from relatively insignificant increments of land resulting from the slow recovery of forest and the draining of marsh lands, the area available to Europeans had remained virtually unchanged. If anything, in fact, it had decreased as a consequence of the encroachment of the Turks into south-east Europe, almost as far as the gates of Vienna. The consequence was, of course, that the population of Europe, pressing hard on the means of subsistence, was also stable, or roughly stable, increasing from around 1100 to 1300, but decreasing again between 1350 and 1450. The rise of empires – the Frankish empire, the Holy Roman Empire, the Bulgarian empire, the northern empire of Canute the Great, and other shorter-lived, more transient empires – did not add to wealth; all they did was to transfer wealth to other hands. Only after the discovery of the New World did this begin to change. The inflow of American treasure, together with the highly profitable voyages to the South Seas – to India, Java, Sumatra, etc. – reversed the long descent of prices and brought about the capital accumulation which eventually made the Industrial Revolution possible. It was the gold and the silver, for example, brought back by Sir Francis Drake in his ship *The Golden Hind* that provided the capital for the two great English trading companies, the East India Company and the Levant Company; and the profits of the merchants in those two companies were invested, particularly at the end of the seventeenth and during the early eighteenth century, in the early industries of England: in the cotton industry of Lancashire, the iron industry of Birmingham, and the potteries of Staffordshire.

Here, then, in the capital accumulated by trade with the Orient, are the origins of the great scientific and technological explosions which put Europe ahead of the rest of the world in the nineteenth century. Of course, the capital did not have to be used in this way. The wealth acquired by trade could have been squandered. It could have been spent on luxury, and undoubtedly much was spent in this way on conspicuous living, on vast houses, on a host of servants, in the same way as by and large it was spent by the aristocracy in India. If this had been all, then Europe no doubt would have continued to stagnate, and there would have been no take-off into modern industrial society. For Europe to make the decisive step forward from an agricultural to an industrial society, something else was needed – another factor, namely, a class or a social group which was ready to use the new opportunities, a mercantile capitalist class. The question, therefore, is why such a class arose in Europe and why it did not arise elsewhere. For what differentiates Europe from the great civilizations of Asia is not, as many European historians have tried to show, some innate European genius arising in some mysterious way from the amalgamation of Greek and Roman and Christian and Germanic virtues; what really differentiates it is the structure of European society. We shall not determine the place of Europe in world history by trying to define the peculiar qualities of the European mind, which perhaps were not so peculiar after all, but by examining the social structure of Europe, by contrast and by comparison with that of the other civilizations of the world.

In my view, therefore, the central fact in the history of Europe is the development of a distinctive social structure, of social forms which are not found, or which are only found to a much smaller extent, elsewhere. In the same way, I believe that the essential stages, or turning points, in the history of Europe are the moments when we can see these new social forms emerging. These, I believe, are the points upon which historians should focus attention. Obviously it would be absurd in a small space to try to give a complete survey of these changes, but I can at least pick out and comment upon a few which seem to me to be particularly important.

First of all, it is important to define what we mean by European history and when European history began. European historians often write as though Europe existed from the very beginning. Except in a crude geological or geographical sense, that simply is not true. Neither Greek society, nor Hellenistic society, nor Roman society, were essentially European societies. The Greek Hellenistic civilization and the Roman Empire which was its successor were essentially Mediterranean civilizations, centred on the Mediterranean Sea. One part of the Roman Empire lay in Europe, concentrated until relatively late in its history south of the Danube, the Alps and the Pyrenees. It was equally powerful in North Africa, which played a far more significant part in its economy. But the axis, and as time passed increasingly the most important focus, of this Mediterranean civilization was in the east, in the area of Asia Minor, Egypt, and as far as the Black Sea. These were the regions where the great cities were located: Alexandria with two million inhabitants, Antioch probably equally large, both the termini of important trade routes linking the Roman Empire with the more advanced civilizations of the Orient. This was the heartland of Roman civilization, which, particularly after the capital was moved from Rome to Constantinople, was far more Eastern than Western in character. Only when Rome fell and the barbarians advanced from the region east of the Carpathians and penetrated into the Roman Empire first across the Danube, and then to Italy and Gaul and through Spain across into North Africa, did the changes begin which transformed a Mediterranean into a European civilization.

The irruption of Germanic and later of Slav barbarians from the steppe-land of Eastern Europe and the rise of Islam were the two decisive events in this process. The great Islamic civilization which emerged from Arabia and spread rapidly through North Africa into Spain – which at the same time advanced in a great encircling movement through Palestine and Asia Minor towards Constantinople, as well as expanding through Persia, into India and South-east Asia – cut off Western Europe from the other centres of world civilization, and shut it in, turning it back upon itself. This without doubt is the beginning of a separate European history.

Even so, it is important not to exaggerate. People at that time did not think of themselves as Europeans; they thought of themselves as Franks, as Bavarians, as Lombards, as Anglo-Saxons, and so on. The idea that all these different peoples form part of one civilization called a European civilization only emerged very late – surprisingly late – probably not before the fifteenth century and not very effectively until the seventeenth century. It would seem that consciousness of Europe as a single entity was a response to the advance of the Ottoman Turks into Europe during the fourteenth century. The sense of European solidarity, which at the same time was a sense of Christian solidarity, was a response to Turkish pressure. Still, the fact remains that the very beginnings, the germ cells, of European society, as distinct from the earlier intercontinental Mediterranean society of Rome, date from the fifth and sixth centuries of the Christian era – the conventional date, though it has no real meaning, is 476 – and the first thing to note is how relatively late on a comparative time scale this is. By the year 500 of the Christian era, China and India were already great civilizations with advanced bureaucratic governments. In Europe, on the contrary, society was still primitive and agricultural. West of Byzantium, there were still societies which did not even understand taxation, societies which were just emerging from the tribal stage, forming small and mostly unstable kingdoms, strikingly different from the great Chinese Empire. In all respects Western Europe lagged behind, just as it lagged behind the great Umayyad Caliphate, which conquered Asia Minor and North Africa, and which, far more than Western Europe, was the intellectual heir of Greece and Rome.

In the centuries that followed, attempts were made to weld this primitive western society into a single empire. They began with the Frankish ruler, Charles the Great, in the year 800, and they were continued after 962 by the German emperors of the Saxon, Salian and Hohenstaufen dynasties. All these attempts to impose a unitary structure on Europe failed, probably because western society – unlike Chinese society – was still too primitive. That is to say, it lacked the resources to build the necessary bureaucratic base, and I suspect that this failure was the first decisive, distinguishing feature of European history. Of course, no one can say what would have happened if it had succeeded; but it is only necessary to compare countries like China or India, where great empires existed, to see the differences. The urge to imperial government was certainly as strong in Europe as it was anywhere else. The Franks and Germans may not have known of China or India; but they certainly knew of the Islamic Caliphate, if only because of the famous elephant which the great Caliph, Harun Al-Rashid, sent as a gift to Charles the Great. But what they always had before their

21

eyes – the example they aspired to follow – was the Roman Empire; and if the Chinese emperors regarded themselves as the Sons of Heaven, it is safe to say that the Western emperors regarded themselves as the stepsons. Certainly they regarded themselves as the intermediaries between their subjects and God. Their conception of their position was entirely theocratic; they regarded religion as a sort of pillar of the state, and looked on the priests – beginning with the High Priest, the pope in Rome – as the servants of their theocracy. If they had succeeded, there is no doubt that they would have created what, not unfairly, may be called a Confucian state – that is to say, a society of an hierarchical, rigid, noncompetitive kind.

At this stage, therefore, there was less divergence between Europe and Asia than is sometimes supposed, except that the European rulers were far less equipped than the emperors of China to put their ideas into practice. The ideal the European rulers were aiming at was basically the same as that of the Chinese and other Oriental rulers. That is why it seems to me that the first great turning point in European history was the upheaval – it lasted for some fifty years between 1076 and 1122 – in which this ideal, this effort to weld the core of Europe into one imperial state, was destroyed. In history books it is usually described as the conflict between empire and papacy, between king and pope, about who should appoint bishops. But this was purely the external side of the matter. In reality it was a conflict between two opposed conceptions of the nature of society, and in particular a conflict for the freedom of the priesthood from the state.

What is significant about this conflict is that the papacy mobilized in its support all those dissident elements which did not wish to be submerged in an imperial theocracy. It turned to France for support against Germany, and the pope himself often took refuge on French soil; it turned to the little countries on the periphery, Denmark, Croatia, Bohemia, which were afraid of being absorbed in the Empire; it turned in particular to the cities – the rising cities of Italy, especially Milan – and won their support. In this way, although the outcome was not finally decided for another century, this struggle really decided that Europe was not to be one empire but was to be a plurality of small states. That, no doubt, was not what the pope intended, any more than it was what the emperor intended; but it was the result of the pope's actions.

In addition, the conflict set up a great intellectual ferment, or what an Indian historian has called a 'polarity of spiritual conflicts'. I think the polarity which arose in this way was the origin of the restlessness or inquisitiveness of the European mind, and of the dialectical approach to knowledge. As a matter of fact, dialectics emerged in the twelfth century in the wake of this great conflict; its best known exponent was the famous French philosopher, Peter Abelard, and Abelard's book, *Sic et Non* (Yes and No), was based on the posing of opposites from which to draw a conclusion.

The importance of all this is that by this means Europe escaped the rigidity which great imperial systems are apt to impose, both on society and on thought. The modern German philosopher, Karl Jaspers, made the essential point when he said that the West did not coagulate into 'a dogmatic fixity of institutions and ideas', that it did not become stabilized. In particular, the European cities – first those of Italy, not only Milan, but the maritime cities of Genoa, Pisa and Palermo, later the cities on the Atlantic seaboard of Spain, but also Marseilles and Barcelona, then the cities of the Netherlands, Ghent, Bruges and Antwerp, and the Hanseatic cities of northern Germany, Hamburg, Bremen, Lübeck and others, which were all great trading centres, and finally the cities of England, London, Bristol, Southampton – were able, because of this conflict between Church and State, to develop in relative freedom, playing off one side against the other. No doubt the cities were freer in some parts of Europe than in others; but compared with other areas all enjoyed relative freedom, and the result was the rise of city-states, or city-republics, which looked after their own affairs in their own way without too much attention to kings and princes and emperors. In particular, they looked after their trading interests and especially their maritime trade. This freedom which grew up in the cities was the source of modern capitalist enterprise.

In saying this, I am not in any way drawing a contrast between the dynamic West and the static East, between what used to be regarded as Oriental stagnation and Western progress. No sensible person today would believe in contrasts of that sort. The civilizations of the East had all the elements for a breakthrough from the ancient type of agricultural society to a capitalist society except one, and that was a new social class of bankers and merchants, powerful enough to direct society into new channels. The volume of commerce was certainly as great in Persia, and in India and in China, as it was in Europe, if not greater. There was also an advanced technology and ample capital. What was lacking was a social structure which gave these potentialities time to expand, and this is the difference I have tried to explain. The difference is that the social structure in Europe favoured these classes and in Asia it did not. It is a startling fact, perhaps an accident of history, that just at the moment when Europe was ready to strike out into the world at the close of the fifteenth century, Asian societies which had been just as thrusting, just as dynamic, suddenly became immobile. After centuries of intense maritime activity the Chinese withdrew from the oceans; shipping between the China Seas and the Persian Gulf came to a halt. Why? This is not the place to discuss the reasons, but it is important to see the contrast. I think the explanation really lies in social differences, in the relative freedom of the small European communities and the rigidity of the great empires, the great imperial cities and the great imperial societies. At all events, China and India, and Japan under the Tokugawa Shogunate, which had all been comparatively expansionary, now withdraw into the shells of their old, traditional cultures; they cut themselves off from a changing external world just when European expansion was beginning.

This contrast is important because it shows that the great expansion of Europe in the world was not due only to developments in Europe as so many European historians have argued. It was due also to the fact that the resistance which had existed to European maritime expansion became weaker and almost ceased. Europe became active just when Asia was becoming inactive, and this difference was also reflected in the intellectual sphere, in intellectual attitudes. In a sense it could not be otherwise. The consolidation and stabilization of the great religions and ethical systems of Asia created a rigid intellectual framework, nowhere, I suppose, more marked than in Confucian China. Hinduism became static, and everywhere the intellectual elite was tied up in its traditionalism. In Europe also, no doubt, if it could have done so, the Church

A world through European eyes

would have imposed equally narrow limits on intellectual speculation, but the Church could not do so. The case of Galileo, for one,
indicates what might have happened. But the Church was ham-
pered by the quarrel of empire and papacy which began at the end
of the eleventh century, and went on until 1250; though this did
not result in a downright victory for either side, it ruined the
prospect of either the State or the Church imposing real control on
thought. The outcome was that intellectually Europeans were
relatively free of shackles and this meant that the spirit of enquiry
could take root.

It took root much more slowly and gradually than European
historians used to maintain. The real change in the intellectual
atmosphere occurred not so much in the sixteenth century at the
time of the Renaissance – I suspect that the importance of the
Renaissance in European history has been considerably exaggerated – but rather in the seventeenth, and essentially in the second
half of that century. Down to around 1650 and 1660 the old confu-
sion, the old interconnection and interrelationship between politics and religion were still very evident in Europe. Hobbes'
Leviathan, published in 1651, is regarded as one of the foundation
stones of modern political theory. But we should never forget that
no less than half of Hobbes' book (the half we do not read) is
concerned with the 'Christian Commonwealth' and 'the kingdom
of Darkness'. After 1660 there was a reorientation and a seculariza-
tion of thought, of which the writings of John Locke are the clearest
evidence. The symbol of this secular change was the foundation in
London, in 1662, of the Royal Society, the great scientific association which still exists today.

This was the next, perhaps the last, great turning point in European history before our own days. We call it the Scientific Revolution, and its symbolic figure was Isaac Newton. Naturally it had its
precursors or prophets, none more outstanding than Francis
Bacon at the beginning of the seventeenth century. In Bacon's
book The New Atlantis, which he published in London in 1626, he
set out in advance with extraordinary clarity what the Scientific
Revolution was about. It meant, he said, 'the knowledge of causes
and secret motions of things, and the enlarging of the bounds of
human empire, to the effecting of all things possible'. It implied, in

25

other words, the belief that the physical and social environments of man are both subject to rational manipulation, and that history and nature, instead of setting a limit to human potentialities, are subject to human will and action and can be moulded by man.

Whether that belief in human potentialities is exaggerated is certainly a question that can be argued. It sums up, nevertheless, the significance of the Scientific Revolution, both in European history and in world history. It is important to note that the Scientific Revolution was first a specifically European revolution in thought, the product of the peculiar conditions of European society as they had developed over a thousand years, with no parallel elsewhere in the seventeenth-century world; but at the same time it was a revolution which had world-wide effects. Secondly, it was the last great turning point in European history before the present, because all the things which made Europe the focal point of historical events from 1815 to 1914 (perhaps until 1939) – its science, its technology, its industrial strength – sprang in the end from the Scientific Revolution.

I have tried in this chapter to set out some of the main turning points of European history when we set it in a world perspective. We see that many of the things that loom large in conventional histories of Europe lose much of their importance in a wider context; in a world perspective, the emphasis shifts and changes. The conventional divisions of European history have little relevance when we look at Europe not by itself but as part of the world. The old division between medieval and modern history in 1492, in particular, has very little meaning. The great change in outlook, the great change in intellectual climate, the change which ushers in the modern world, comes not with the Renaissance or the Reformation but with the Scientific Revolution of the seventeenth century. The modern history of Europe, in other words, starts not in 1485 or 1492 but between 1660 and 1680. In fact, it might be argued that there were only two great breaks in European history: the one at the end of the eleventh century when Europe, which had been hemmed in from all sides by the Saracens, the Vikings and the Magyars, broke out and began to expand. The second came at the end of the seventeenth century when the scientific spirit, which was the mark of Europe in modern times, really took shape.

The impact of Europe on the world between 1500 and 1700 was far smaller than many people think. It was marginal or peripheral, touching only the coastline of Asia, and then at scattered points. It was only when its new science and the practical application of its new science in technology carried it forward in the latter part of the eighteenth century that Europe left an imprint on the rest of the world. Today, the science and the technology which originated in Europe have become part of the equipment of all the world's peoples, of mankind everywhere; Europeans have no copyright in them and the fact that they originated in Europe does not prevent their being universal. Nevertheless, they revolutionized the world and in the next chapter I shall try to analyse their impact and what that has done to a world which scientifically and technologically, if not politically, it has made one.

Technology –
servant or master?

2

The beginning of modern history – I am talking now of world history, not just of European history – lies in the Scientific Revolution in the middle and the second half of the seventeenth century, which I discussed briefly at the end of the preceding chapter. In Japan, modern history is dated from the Meiji Restoration in 1868. The conventional starting point of Chinese modern history is the Opium War between 1839 and 1842. This seems to me to be as superficial and parochial, from a world historical point of view, as the habit of European historians of dating modern European history from the French Revolution in 1789. These are important dates from a national point of view; they are not so important from a world point of view. What has shaped our world, created the world we know, in London, in New York, in Tokyo, is the impact of science and technology. The years 1868 in Japan, 1842 in China are significant because they mark the decision, after some two centuries of self-imposed isolation and withdrawal, to come to terms in one way or another with this ineluctable fact. In one way or another, I say, because the Chinese response was confused, ambiguous, half-hearted, whereas in Japan after Commodore Perry 'knocked on the door' in 1854 – not immediately, of course, but very quickly – the decision was taken to appropriate western science and use it for Japanese purposes.

The result is that today Japan is the world's third industrial power, outdistanced only by the two great transcontinental superpowers with their immense resources. But the basic fact was the existence of a science and a technology to which in the long run Japan and China, and of course other countries as well, had to respond whether they wanted to or not. They could no longer opt out, because their science and technology gave Europeans and Americans such a leverage in the world that they could force other countries thousands of miles away to open their doors whether they wanted to or not. The advance of science and technology, whose origins we can trace back to seventeenth-century Europe, was bound by its very nature to be universal. This seems to me its distinctive feature. It could never be contained in watertight national compartments, but precisely because it was scientific it was universal in its application.

The Scientific Revolution of the seventeenth century seems remote and is remote. It is a long way from 1660 to the present, and I have no intention – even if I were technically equipped to do so – of providing a history of these 300 years of scientific and technological advance. All that needs to be said, I think, is that this advance occurred in four distinct stages.

The first stage covers the century from 1660 to 1760. At this time interest in science was speculative and theoretical rather than practical. The second stage begins around 1760 and goes on more or less to 1860, and may be identified with the first phase of the Industrial Revolution. In this second stage science and technology were used, in the main, to improve existing processes, to mechanize them, to speed them up, but very little that was new in principle was introduced. The power loom, for example, worked more efficiently than the hand loom – it could do more work, produce more cloth in a given time, but it embodied no really new principle. Naturally the use of steam power did have social consequences as well. It meant that instead of taking work home, workers went into factories. It meant also change and hardship. In Europe, for example, the hand-loom weavers of Silesia were thrown out of work by the cheaper machine-produced cloth of England. In the same way in Asia, the Indian textile industry suffered from the competition of Lancashire cotton. While we should not minimize the changes that took place at this early stage, the fact remains that, down to the middle of the nineteenth century, they were fairly slow and, for most people, very gradual in their effect on the quality and tempo of life.

It was in the next and third stage, after about 1860 or 1870, that the really revolutionary effects of science and technology were felt. Not only were there radically new inventions, things completely unheard of, unthought of in the past – wireless telegraphy, for example, and electric lighting, the internal combustion engine, the telephone, to name only a few – but this stage was revolutionary also in its effects on people's lives. The first stage of the Industrial Revolution had been a revolution of coal and iron. The second stage, the stage after 1870, was a revolution of steel, electricity and chemicals. Up to the middle of the nineteenth century, steel had been almost a semi-precious metal; the total world production was only around 80,000 tons. With the introduction of new scientific processes the output rose by 1900 to 28 million tons. But the point is that steel made it possible to manufacture stronger, finer, more precise instruments, so that steel became itself the basis for further progress. The impact of electricity was even more spectacular. As late as 1850, no one could possibly have predicted that electricity would be used on a large scale as a source of power; but after Siemens' invention of the dynamo in 1867, the pace of advance was extraordinarily quick. Already by 1882 the world's first electric power plant was opened in New York, and when electric power passed into common usage the whole face of the world was changed. To assess its impact we only have to recall Lenin's famous remark: 'Communism equals Soviet power plus electrification'.

The fourth (and so far the final) stage of the Scientific Revolution has been even more remarkable in its consequences. It is barely thirty years old but its effects are all around us, visible for everyone to see. Its most striking symbol, the one of which we are all conscious, is nuclear fission, the great atomic cloud rising high above Hiroshima, the use of nuclear energy for war and for peaceful purposes. Its other symbol, the symbol of man's age-old longing to conquer the heavens, is the spaceship, the space satellite making for the moon and beyond. But the essentials are perhaps a little more prosaic, though they also are stupendous enough. The revolution through which we are living is often called the electronic revolution and there is every reason to think that electronics and automation and the computer will affect our lives even more profoundly in a few years than either the first Industrial Revolution or the great scientific changes at the close of the nineteenth century. For, after all, the important thing for us as human beings is not simply to register the progress of science and technology, but rather to measure, at every stage, its impact on us and on our environment.

What, then, has been its impact? There are in all countries and in most large cities museums of science and technology where we are asked to admire the marvels of modern science; and of course they are marvellous and we have every reason to admire them as the products of human intellect and human ingenuity. It would be ridiculous to suggest otherwise. But machines in themselves are one thing, machines as instruments of social change are another. Obviously not all machines, not all scientific discoveries have wide-ranging general effects. The sight of the first Sputnik high in the skies may have stimulated our imagination. It certainly stimulated mine when I saw it crossing the horizon one clear night in Colorado. But it did not directly affect me in my daily life, and that is why a machine such as the electronic computer seems to me much more characteristic of the present stage of technological innovation than the spaceship. One automobile is a curiosity. We may stop and look at it, as people no doubt did in the early days between 1900 and 1910; we may admire it, perhaps desire it, but it does not really affect our daily life. Ten million automobiles in one country – that is something quite different. It is a social fact. We no longer stare, we no longer admire, we take them for granted; but they affect the whole quality of our lives. In fact we may become dependent on them, we may become their servants instead of their being, as they are intended to be, our servants. That is what Emerson meant many years ago when he said that 'things are in the saddle and ride the world'.

The essential point is that, in the space of a century, probably a good deal less than a century, our lives – the lives of everyone everywhere, with a few minimal exceptions, even the lives (I imagine) of people in Iceland and Outer Mongolia – have been totally transformed by science and technology. And, unless we are submerged by a global catastrophe, it is an irreversible process. We all tend to think in terms of machines. That is how we instinctively think of science and technology. Perhaps it is a natural thing to do, but it is also misleading. If we turn back now to what I called the third stage of the Scientific Revolution, to the period roughly after 1870, what was every bit as important as the invention of new processes and new machines was the progress achieved in medicine, hygiene and nutrition. At a time when industry was bringing people from the countryside to the cities in ever-increasing numbers, this was a question of inestimable importance. Modern industrial society as we know it today would have been impossible without it. If we are going to have great urban centres with populations of a quarter of a million or half a million, of a million or two millions, we are faced immediately with the problem of epidemics and the problem of feeding. Only the progress of science made it possible to cope with those problems. The great age of bacteriology, which is associated with the names of Pasteur and Koch, began after 1870 and made it possible to control the old scourges of mankind, such as cholera. The use of antiseptics, first employed on a large scale by Lister in Glasgow in 1865 – Glasgow at that time was a foul and filthy city – was the basis of modern hygiene, which made the great urban centres habitable. Pasteur's work on sterilization led, from around 1890, not only to the pasteurization of milk but more generally to the bulk conservation of foodstuffs and the provision of cheap and steady supplies of food for the growing world population. Refrigeration made it possible to provide adequate meat supplies for the cities – after 1876 refrigerator wagons brought chilled meat from Kansas City to New York and refrigerated ships carried it further on to Europe. Argentine beef became available in London in 1877, mutton from New Zealand in 1882. Equally important was the food canning industry, which was made possible only through new processes of tin plating. The sale of canned vegetables was only 400,000 cases in 1870; it had grown by 1914 to 55 million cases.

The reason I have emphasized these less spectacular sides of the scientific and technological and industrial revolution, the ones which we take for granted as if they were always there, is because cumulatively they are the aspects which have the most immediate impact on our lives. The other fundamental fact which cannot be exaggerated is the impact of medical science on the world's population. In some ways, perhaps, no modern discovery was more important than Sir Ronald Ross's identification in 1897 of the mosquito as the carrier of malaria. The control of diseases such as cholera and malaria, which had killed off human beings in millions through the ages, in combination with medical skill in reducing infant mortality and the rapidly increasing expectation of life, produced a demographic revolution on a world scale which is undoubtedly the most distinctive feature of the present age. Hitherto the world's population had been held down everywhere, in all civilizations, at all times, by famine and disease. Now, as a result of the advance of medical science, together with the introduction of new scientific agricultural techniques, the population went ahead by leaps and bounds. In Japan, for example, the population seems to have been more or less static and stable for a century and a half before 1870. Then in the next sixty years, between 1870 and 1930, mainly as a result of the declining mortality rate, the population of Japan doubled.

Of course, the Japanese experience was not exceptional. The population surge had even more dramatic effects in India, China and Africa. Here the rate of increase was far higher. And the other significant fact is the increasing tempo of population growth. For example, in the period of thirty years between 1920 and 1950, the world's population increased by 37 per cent – roughly, that is, by 12 per cent each decade. In the next ten years, between 1950 and 1960, it increased by 21 per cent; and there is no present sign of its slowing down. This increasing tempo is the reason why population or over-population has become one of the over-riding problems of the contemporary world, and there are already prophecies, perhaps pessimistic, that if nothing is done to stem it, by the end of the present century the world's population will have outgrown the world's resources and there will be an overwhelming catastrophe.

The point is that none of this merely 'happened' by a steady, normal evolution of human history. It is the result of a scientific and technological revolution which has no precedent in any past civilization. It is true, and historians rightly emphasize the fact, that from the very beginning of historic time, technological change has played a dominant part in history. Historians speak, for example, of a neolithic agricultural revolution, and obviously the discovery of new agricultural techniques, such as the plough, and later the substitution of the heavy plough which could turn the soil for the light plough which simply scratched and tilled the surface of the soil, played a decisive role in man's permanent struggle with his environment. The discovery of the use of flints for arrowheads, making hunting for foodstuffs more effective, more 'scientific', the discovery of metals such as iron and bronze, and their use for implements – these are all stages in the history of mankind. That is why we speak of the Bronze Age, the Iron Age, the Industrial Age, etc.

The beginning of agriculture, which implied the creation of agricultural technology, however primitive it may have been, was obviously a great turning point in human history. It meant that man, instead of being nomadic, instead of wandering from place to place in search of foodstuffs, settled down to cultivate the soil. It was the beginning of human settlements – farms, villages and ultimately towns and cities. If we think of human history as ultimately the conquest of man's environment – the provision of food, the provision of shelter, of warmth, of clothing – technology was always basic. Technology also underlay the division of labour – one man tilling the land, one weaving cloth, another providing protection – which is at the root of all civilization. Science in its broadest sense, technology, has always been there – it is what lifted us from the savages, from the other animals. As such, it is a basic fact of human history.

Nevertheless, the Scientific Revolution which shapes our lives today is different, qualitatively as well as quantitatively. It is not merely that the number and speed of scientific discoveries have been infinitely greater, that more has been crowded into one century than into the preceding two thousand years, or that the changes introduced by scientific and technological innovation have been far more spectacular. Their character also has been different. In the first stage of the Industrial Revolution, as I have pointed out, the innovations were mainly improvements of existing processes. They were also mainly the discoveries of practical men, men who had little if any real scientific training or knowledge of pure science. The basic fact was the discovery of steam power – or rather, since the existence of steam power was known, the discovery of how to use it in industry, to substitute it for horsepower and human power. This stage of the Industrial Revolution fits in with the earlier stages of technological advance – it is only an extension of them. The steam engine (even, as a matter of fact, the automobile) is not different in principle from the horse-drawn chariot – both depend on the age-old discovery of the wheel. But the later stages of the Industrial Revolution are quite different, because they spring from a real mastery of scientific knowledge, of 'pure' science. This time it was not merely an industrial revolution but, quite specifically, a scientific revolution. It was scientific in the sense that few of its main achievements could have been discovered simply by the application of common sense or new materials. In chemistry, in electricity, in electronics, in nuclear physics, it implied a knowledge of scientific principles which are increasingly complex, increasingly sophisticated. In other words, it adds a new dimension, a dimension of pure theory, of deduction from first principles, of scientific thinking.

It is in this sense that one can legitimately say that the Scientific Revolution ushered in a new phase in man's history, a phase without precedent, and which for the first time in history has made the whole world one. Formerly, you could have great scientific discoveries in China which remained unknown in western Europe just as you could have great scientific discoveries in western Europe which remained unknown in China. Today that is not the case. Despite, for example, all the efforts of the Americans to retain the secrets of the atom bomb and the hydrogen bomb, they were the common knowledge of scientists all over the world in a very few years. That is what we mean when we say that science has created one world civilization obliterating most of the age-old differences of peoples and races. I am not suggesting that the results have been uniformly good – undoubtedly, valuable traditions have been lost in the process. All I have tried to do, without making value judgments, is to show in broad outline what has happened.

Nevertheless, we cannot rest content with a mere account of

what happened. What are the implications of the Scientific Revolution? When we ask this question – and naturally it is the question that concerns us most of all – inevitably we move away from historical facts and enter a realm of speculation. When we move on from the historical facts, it is only fair to say, from the outset, that my views are no more authoritative than those of my readers – in many cases probably less so. I can only offer my conclusions for what they are worth. Of course, in so far as the Scientific Revolution in its modern form is now more than a hundred years old, we can see some of its implications or consequences, as they have worked themselves out since the closing years of the nineteenth century, and that provides us with a useful guide. But it is never entirely safe to 'extrapolate', to take a trend which we think we can see developing in the recent past and project it into the future. Only thirty years ago, for example, the general view, not only among the general public but also among experts, was that the trend in population in Europe and North America was downwards, that population was decreasing, that the net reproduction rate was falling below equilibrium. That projection has proven to be wrong, and it is a warning to us to be very careful before we say that something which has been happening, let us say, for fifteen or twenty years (which after all is a mere speck of time in human history) will go on happening in the same way in the future. Moreover, when we talk about implications it is very hard to keep to the facts and to exclude our own hopes, our own fears, and our own prejudices.

Nevertheless, there are one or two things we can say which I think are more or less indisputable.

First, the Scientific Revolution and its social consequences, short of a catastrophe, are irreversible. By that I mean that we can only go forward. Certainly we cannot go backward and I do not think we can even just stand still. Of course, if there were a catastrophe – if, for example, there were a third world war with atomic weapons – we must expect a decimation of the world's population, with all its consequences. But destruction on that scale would really be the end of civilization as we know it. It would presumably mean a fresh start on a new foundation, not necessarily, I think, a return to barbarism – let us say to the position of the human race 10,000 or

15,000 years ago – but certainly a return to much simpler conditions, to altogether lower and simpler standards of living. This would put a premium on the less advanced and more remote peoples because they are better able to adapt themselves to primitive conditions, and it would be almost impossible for the more civilized, because they have become used to the ease and refinements of civilized living and I think, in many cases, simply could not exist without them.

But short of a catastrophe on that scale – and the results of that are really beyond prediction – the simple fact is that our lives are so attuned to science that we cannot do without it. The world which science has created is so complex, the population to feed and take care of is so immense, that it requires all the resources of science and technology. That seems to me irrefutable. The simpler societies of only two or three generations ago have gone beyond recall. Those who remember them may sometimes regret their disappearance and the loss at any rate of some of their qualities. But nothing can be done about it – we cannot put the clock back. We live in a scientific world and all we can do, or all we can try to do, is to make the best and not the worst of it.

Secondly, the impact of science and technology is indivisible. That is to say, we must take it as a whole. Much as we might like to, we cannot say that we will have the automobile, the washing machine, the refrigerator, the television, but not the hydrogen bomb. We cannot put limits on scientific inquiry without risking its drying up, and so great is our dependence on it we dare not do that. Also, just as important, we cannot will the end without the means. If we are to have cheap, plentiful, mass-produced goods – television, let us say, or simply such essentials as food and clothing in adequate quantity and adequate variety – then we must have the form of society which produces such goods. That is to say, we must have a factory system, we must have the urban agglomerations which go with the factory system, we must have an industrial society with all its characteristic features, with its own forms, for example, of recreation and amusement, television and the cinema, organized sport and the like.

Already by the end of the nineteenth century this fact was becoming evident. The great Krupps Steel Works in Germany, for instance, employed only 122 men in 1846. By 1873 it had 16,000 on its payroll, by 1913 almost 70,000. The new industrial technology necessitated the creation of large-scale undertakings and that meant the concentration of the population in vast urban agglomerations within reach of the factory. In this way the whole physiognomy, the whole physical appearance, of the industrialized countries was changed. So, secondly, were social relations. In a small business, let us say, of five or ten men, there could still be and still often was a direct relationship between the employer and the employee, but when the workers increased to thousands and tens of thousands, they became simply numbers, or 'hands'. In this way, the new industrial technology created what is today called 'mass society'. In a sense, it was a vicious circle. Science and technology created the new industrial society; and then, to keep the new industrial society going, to keep the wheels turning round, to make them work more smoothly, more efficiently, more science and more technology were needed. As I said, there is really no calling a halt, there is no point at which we can say enough and no more.

No one, I think, can possibly maintain that the results, for the ordinary man and woman at least, for the ordinary worker, have not been beneficial. On this rather controversial ground I should, I suppose, say beneficial 'on the whole', beneficial 'in the long run'. In the early stages of the Industrial Revolution, conditions in the factories were dreadful. Towns were filthy and unhygienic, hours of work were incredibly long, wages were terribly low and relations between owners and workers and the treatment of workers by management were anything but good. Perhaps that was inevitable to begin with, perhaps it was a stage which had to be endured. Be that as it may, everyone knows that the situation today has changed. Maybe it has not changed as much as we should like, but it has changed profoundly – as regards conditions and hours of work, as regards wages, as regards benefits. But when I say that the results of the Scientific Revolution have been beneficial for ordinary men and women, I am thinking of bigger things even than that. For one thing, the expectation of life has increased immensely. Life is no longer, as Hobbes described it in the seventeenth century, 'nasty, brutish and short'. Women have ceased to be drudges, tied to an incessant round of pregnancies and child-birth, which in the past wore them out prematurely. In general, standards of living are far higher for a far larger number of people and this improvement has not been purchased, as it almost always was in the past, by reducing the standard of living oı other people. As we have seen in China, the famines which until quite recently wiped out millions have been banished in most parts of the world; so have the terrible, disfiguring epidemics – leprosy and the rest – which again, until recently, left a wreckage of maimed human beings fit for nothing but begging. As a result of science, of nothing else but science, material progress has been immense, and though material progress does not necessarily result in moral or intellec-tual progress, we must surely agree that it is the precondition of them. That is to say, people living on the very edge of subsistence have no time for anything else but scraping by as best they can; they have no time for intellectual pursuits and precious little inter-est in morality.

It is true, of course, that some of those who were relatively well off in the past, the comfortable middle classes, have bemoaned the consequences of industrialization. They regret what they call its levelling effects, the uniformity and standardization it introduces. It is not difficult for me to understand that because in a sense I am one of them, and when I look back to the 1920s and even dimly to my childhood before 1914, it is impossible sometimes not to be a little nostalgic. But nostalgia is a bad guide, and one has to recog-nize that what may have been the 'good old times' for one section of society were the 'bad old times' for another. For the ordinary person, for the person without inherited means, the world is an infinitely better place to live in at the present than it was in 1913, and we owe this in most essential ways to science and to the practical application of science and technology.

In saying this, I am not unaware that technology poses its own problems. Who could expect otherwise? Unfortunately, we cannot have the benefits of science without the attendant risks. What can be used can always be abused, and so, after a period in which people were carried away by the infinite potentialities of science, we seem to have entered in the last ten or fifteen years a period in which it has become the fashion to question the benefits of science and to pick out its alleged evils. No one in his senses would under-rate them, and they certainly are something we cannot afford to ignore. It is a fact that we have it in our power to destroy the world as a habitable planet. It is a fact that we are beset all over the world by environmental problems which go beyond mere amenities – such things as the unpleasantness of great scrap heaps, the pollu-tion of rivers and lakes and seas so that we can no longer safely bathe in them, the air so polluted by fumes that it is unhealthy to breathe, water that is dangerous to drink, food that is affected by pesticides, etc. These things, of course, are disagreeable but they only scratch the surface. Far more serious is the way we are inter-fering with the whole balance of nature, through insecticides, through nuclear waste, through radioactive isotopes, through chlorinated hydrocarbons, interfering in ways we simply do not know, do not understand and of which we cannot foresee the results. So that what is at stake in the ecological crisis we face today is the very capacity of the earth to sustain advanced forms of life. Already the world's fisheries are in danger – only recently certain species of seafood such as clams were banned in New England as dangerous to eat, and shoals of herring have been washed up dead. In addition, the voracious appetite of industry is using up the world's resources, particularly its mineral resources, at the most terrifying speed.

Facts such as these, and many more, are indisputable. The important thing is that we should put the responsibility where it lies. Because we live in a scientific, technological society – because science and technology are the things which distinguish our societies from earlier societies – it is easy to blame science for everything that is wrong. It might be much more rational to blame society. Of course it is true that if scientists had not, for example, invented insecticides, the situation would not have arisen which led to the decision in certain countries to prohibit the use of DDT. But the indiscriminate use of DDT and similar pesticides with all the consequences for insect life, for bird life, ultimately for human life – this is not the responsibility of science. If I mention the profit motive I shall probably be accused of political prejudice. But everyone knows that pollution is largely a matter of cost, that the reason pollutants are discharged into the air or rivers or lakes is because it is the cheapest method of disposal, that the producer who goes out of his way to install anti-pollution devices will (it is often said) soon be 'out of business'.

What we are up against, therefore, is not science but the exploitation of science and technology in anti-social ways. That is not a political statement – the facts are admitted by people everywhere – though the question how best to remedy this situation is no doubt a political question. But that is not the question I am discussing here and now. All I am insisting on is the simple fact that science and technology can be used either in social or in anti-social ways and it is our business to see that they are used in social ways. The reason this is our business is that our whole future, the future of our children, perhaps even the future of the human race, depends upon it. The way forward is not by rejecting science and technology, not by turning against them, but by harnessing them, as they have not really been harnessed in the last fifty years, to definite social ends and social objectives.

There is no doubt that this implies a far more critical approach than is usual to what is commonly called the affluent society, to the modern consumer technocracies with their concentration on growth for its own sake, on conspicuous consumption or (to put it somewhat more bluntly) on sheer wilful waste, with their continuous output of unnecessary goods and often their neglect of the real necessities. What is needed is a better allocation of scientific and technological resources. But science still remains, as it has been from the earliest known times, the crucial tool, and in society as it is shaped today I think the only effective tool, for forging a humane and reasonable future. We cannot retreat from it even if we want to, and most people do not want to. From the time of the neolithic revolution thousands of years ago, technological advance has been the major factor lightening man's burden, making it easier to wring a livelihood from nature, cutting down the sheer physical effort needed. Without it we should still be primitive savages. It has given us the tools to do the job. It cannot do the job for us. In a sense, science is neutral, and it depends on us which side it comes down on. It can destroy us, or it can make a better future; but in either event it is here to stay, shaping our lives every minute of the day and of the night.

Europe and the underdeveloped world

3

The scientific and technological revolution is rapidly creating a world civilization. I do not mean by this that there are no regional variations – I hope they will always exist. None of us wants a totally uniform, totally standardized world. But the very nature of technological societies enforces certain basic uniformities – a hydroelectric dam in Utah, a hydroelectric dam in China, a hydroelectric dam on the River Volta in Africa, or in England, are all much the same. So also is the nuclear reactor. The great metropolises of the world, the cities which are the hub of industrial civilization, have an increasingly similar appearance. The high-rise buildings, the large apartment blocks, the very materials used for construction, are not much different in Düsseldorf in West Germany, in Boston in the United States, in Tokyo, in Hongkong or even in Moscow. A small minority of people everywhere, even in Europe, still affect traditional dress deliberately to emphasize their differences. Wearing African dress is a symbol of African nationalism, just as wearing Bavarian or Silesian dress in Germany is a symbol of the old regional differences in that country; but most people everywhere wear the same sort of clothes with only minor differences of style. Look at a picture of Roosevelt, Stalin and Churchill at the Yalta Conference, or of Mao in his regulation cloth cap; each is different, but the basic pattern is the same. On the Stock Exchanges in London, Tokyo and New York people are not only doing the same things in the same way but they are all wearing the same sort of clothes. And it goes without saying that the workers assembling automobiles in factories and plants in Detroit in the United States, in Cowley or Luton in England, in the Toyota or Datsun works in Japan, the Volkswagen works in West Germany, or the Fiat works in Italy, and also in the great new Fiat plant in the Soviet Union, are all basically performing the same routine.

These regularities, which cut across nations, geographical barriers, different ideologies and political systems, and race, are an essential characteristic of modern civilization. They are perhaps its main differentiating feature, they are what distinguishes it from the civilizations of the past. Nevertheless, it is also true that the impact of science and technology has been and still is uneven. In Europe, particularly in Western Europe, it has a long history. It goes back at least until the latter part of the eighteenth century, and the changes it brought about were then gradually assimilated. In Asia and Africa the impact was far more sudden and therefore more revolutionary. It came from outside rather than from within and often, in fact nearly always, it hit traditional societies which were ill-equipped and ill-adapted to meet it. Often, of course, they were hostile to it because they feared it would operate as a solvent of the existing social order. Japan, I suppose, was unique among the countries of the non-European world in being prepared to meet the challenge and to respond positively to the impact of the new science and technology.

The very fact that the impact of science and technology was sudden and revolutionary also meant that it produced tensions. It produced internal tensions in the traditional societies upon which it fell – nowhere perhaps more marked than in China during the last fifty years of the Ch'ing dynasty because the highly civilized Chinese were well aware of its consequences. But tension was just as evident in all traditional societies from the Arab countries of North Africa to India and Indo-China, the Malayan peninsula and the islands of Indonesia. Secondly, because it was brought by Europeans from outside, because it was regarded, quite correctly at that stage, as a European introduction and a concomitant of European rule and European expansion, it created tensions between the peoples of Asia and Africa and the Europeans. The

Europeans were its beneficiaries, or so the other peoples of the world believed; the peoples of Asia and Africa were its victims. Europeans had a great deal to say at the close of the nineteenth century about the boons and benefits and advantages they were conferring on the rest of the world. It was their justification for their imperial expansion. But no one in his senses, and certainly no Chinese, imagined that the Europeans had travelled halfway around the world just in order to confer benefits on them. Europeans who knew the real position – for example Sir Robert Hart in China – warned the Western governments that the policies of imperialism were dangerous. They predicted the growth of an anti-European movement that was destined to turn into fanaticism and (as one critic said) to 'find expression in the wildest rage'. And in fact, already in the last twenty years of the nineteenth century, there was evidence enough of the incipient revolt against the West: the Senussi War in Tunisia after the establishment of a French Protectorate in 1881, the revolt of Arabi Pasha in Egypt, the Ashanti Rising in the Gold Coast in Africa, the Boxer Rebellion in China in 1900. All these were signs of resistance and opposition. But the European powers, convinced of their technological superiority, particularly their superiority in weapons and in armaments, paid very little attention. Only the success of Japan in 1905 in the war with Russia – a victory which was hailed by the dependent peoples everywhere as a blow to European ascendancy and as proof that European arms were not invincible – produced a change. The result was that by 1914 there were radical and revolutionary groups, small groups but active, in most countries of Asia and the Arab world, which were ready to take the lead against European imperialism.

The impact of western science and technology was the more dramatic because of its suddenness. It is still usual to regard the expansion of Europe as a steady, gradual process, which began in the fifteenth century, until the whole world, step by step, was encompassed by it. But that is hardly an accurate picture. The Indian historian Panikkar coined the phrase 'The Age of Vasco Da Gama' (after the great Portuguese voyager and navigator at the end of the fifteenth century) to cover the whole period of 450 years from 1498 to 1947 as an epoch of European expansion and domination. Other Asian historians have pointed out the element of exaggeration in this description. Actually for 250 years, between 1500 and roughly 1750, the impact of Europe was marginal. The European voyagers only touched the continent of Africa at a few points on the coast, and the same was true in Java, Sumatra, and India. They did not interfere in the internal economies of Asian and African societies, but simply negotiated for commercial rights and privileges with the established authorities. The great interior spaces, the whole interior of Asia and Africa, were left untouched. An Indian historian has rightly pointed out that, if in 1750 the Europeans had withdrawn from the trading stations they had set up on the Asian and African coasts, they would have left little trace other than a few relics of purely antiquarian interest.

What this means is that the effective period of European intervention for most of Africa and Asia actually began only after 1750, and often very much later. The whole interior of Africa, even its geography, was unknown to Europeans until the travels of Stanley and Livingstone in the 1860s and 1870s. For most Africans, therefore, contact with Europeans only occurred during the last quarter of the nineteenth century. In Asia, as is well known, both Japan and China pursued a deliberate policy of exclusion for many generations. In fact long after the treaty ports of China along the coast and up the Yellow River were opened to Europeans and Americans – a process which only began after 1842 – the Chinese peasant, deep in the interior, went on leading his traditional way of life. It was only after 1949 that he was finally brought into the mainstream.

The European impact therefore varied from area to area. African traders in the towns of the Gold and Ivory Coasts were in contact with Europeans from the fifteenth or sixteenth century. So were the traders of Sumatra and Java. But in the interior the old dynasties continued to rule. It was not the impact of the Europeans, but the impact of Europeans armed with all the techniques of modern science, particularly armed with modern weapons, that brought about the fundamental changes. In India in the eighteenth century English merchants were suppliants for the favours of the Mogul emperors. It was when they went with modern weapons and trained military forces that the roles were reversed. The victories of

Clive in India and of Napoleon in Egypt, both in fact with armies far inferior in numbers but far superior in armaments and discipline, really marked the turning point. They marked the superiority of Europe over Asia, both in economic efficiency and in military power. But even so (and this is an important point) material superiority was not equated with moral superiority. Napoleon, for example, still treated his opponents in Egypt on a footing of equality. It was later, in the second half of the nineteenth century, that Europeans began to think that their technical efficiency proved their moral superiority, and was evidence of the greater virtues of European civilization. And it was this claim to moral superiority, to the right to impose European values, that quite rightly provoked Asian and African resentment and revolt. Not European expansion as such but the new imperialism which set in after 1882, with its arrogance, its high-flown pretensions, its self-assurance, and its sense of mission, was the seed-bed of the anti-European, anti-Western, anti-white movement, of the 'race war' which became world-wide after 1947.

There was a second outstanding difference between the old and the new imperialism. In the earlier phase the Europeans naturally influenced Asian and African societies at the few points where they came in contact with them, but the old traditional societies continued to exist as before. European influence did not interfere with their functioning. After 1870 it was different. Under European pressure, particularly when the Europeans displaced the old ruling dynasties as the British and the Dutch and the French did in India, in Indonesia and Indo-China – when they took over direct political control – then the whole social structure was affected and the local societies began to disintegrate.

Even where (as in most of British Africa) the Europeans were content with 'indirect rule' – where they kept the tribal chiefs in power (or at least such chiefs as would cooperate) and ruled through them – the result was much the same. What happened was a two-sided process. On the one side the destruction of the economic substructure of the old society, the erosion of the authority of the old ruling classes, the transformation of considerable elements of the population, deprived of their traditional livelihood, into servants or employees of the foreigner, the loosening of the old social bonds as these people left their homes and traditional occupations and went off to look for alternative work, and ultimately their transformation into an urban and industrial proletariat. That is the one side. On the other, what happened was the remodelling of the economy under the impetus of European enterprise and European investment, which almost inevitably meant that it was made to subserve European interests; in other words, the creation of real colonial economies providing raw materials for European industry. For example, rubber was produced in Indonesia and Malaya, oil was exported from the Middle East, minerals, particularly copper, were mined in Rhodesia and the Congo. The result was that the economies of the by now dependent countries became dependent economies. They were dependent on world markets, on the changing requirements of European manufacturers and on the vagaries of European consumers. And since economic changes of this magnitude are for all practical purposes irreversible, the position in many parts of the ex-colonial world is still the same today, even after independence. Politically a country may become independent but economically it remains tied to the European cartwheel.

Many of these changes had occurred in Europe itself at an earlier stage. In England in the second half of the eighteenth century there was a similar dislocation of the old agrarian society, a similar shift from traditional occupations to new industries, and a drift of population from the countryside into the industrial cities. All change has terrible costs for those involved in it, and in this respect the Asian and African countries, when they were thrown into the vortex of industrialization, were not unique. But there were two differences between their experience and that of Europeans. The first was that, in Asia and in Africa, changes which in Europe had been spread out over five or six generations, changes which had been slowly prepared, were suddenly thrust upon Asia and Africa within fifty or sixty years, and in many cases, often crowded within a single lifetime. That is to say, they were propelled suddenly without preparation out of an age-old traditional way of life into a totally different society. Secondly, the agents of this change were foreigners, people who had very little understanding of the societies with which they were interfering and even less sympathy with the victims of change. No wonder that the result was an anti-Western movement, a wave of resentment against the West which still has not died down.

At first it was a blind resentment, an instinctive explosion of fanatic resistance which came from the heart of the old society, often heroic but always hopeless. Against the immense technical superiority of the Europeans, blind, desperate reactions such as the Boxer Rebellion in China stood no chance. Indeed, in many ways they simply made things worse. The only way to defeat the West was to copy the West, to take over not only Western technologies but also Western forms of political organization, and turn them against the West. It was a very hard lesson to learn. Only Japan embarked systematically on a policy of westernization. Elsewhere, all sorts of compromises were attempted. It was still hoped that it might be possible to take over Western science but retain the old social ethos, as if you could have science without the sort of society in which scientific achievement is at home. In China in particular the path of modernization was hesitant, slow, confused right down to 1949.

Nevertheless, without going into detail, it is safe to say that the decisive fact everywhere was the displacement of traditional elites, the Moslem Mullah, the Brahmin priest, the Chinese Mandarin, the Buddhist monk, by a new elite drawn for the most part from the Western-educated intelligentsia, an elite which assumed the leadership of a revolutionary nationalist, modernist movement, an elite which advocated radical political and social reform and had learned how to manipulate the politics of mass opinion and mass revolt. This was the generation of leaders who led the independence movements and who emerged after 1947 as the first generation of rulers in the newly independent states: Nehru in India, Ho Chi-Minh in Vietnam, Sukarno in Indonesia, Kwame Nkrumah in Ghana.

There was a certain euphoria caused by the revolt against the West which swept over Asia and Africa between 1947 and 1960, a blindness to the hard, inexorable economic facts of life. The assumption was that European interests had stood between the dependent countries of Asia and Africa and their development – that progress, for example, had been prevented by the draining off of the surplus profits for the benefit of European investors, and that once the colonial yoke had been removed they would surge forward. There was also a belief that they could exploit the Cold War, the great conflict dividing the white world in which the Afro-Asian nations at Bandung proclaimed their neutrality, to extort concessions, loans, aid from one side or the other, and preferably, of course, from both. For a short time this worked, but even when it did, it was soon clear that foreign loans and foreign aid touched only the fringe of the problems facing the newly emancipated countries. The Bandung Conference took place in 1955. Ten years later the realities were becoming apparent – and they were bleak realities. In particular, it was seen that economic backwardness was not something that could be spirited away by the wave of a magic wand.

In part, there is no doubt, backwardness was a result of the policies of the colonial powers; but in the 1960s there was little profit in bemoaning this fact in a frenzy of anti-imperialism. Denunciations of imperialism would not cure the problems. In any case, in many parts of Asia and Africa standards of living had always been deplorably low, quite apart from colonialism. Incomes per head in the population were incredibly small and, as things were, these countries could never really have the sort of prosperous consumer society upon which modern industry depends. Moreover, it was seen that mere investment in modern industrial plant was not in itself enough. The way out of backwardness was not merely through machines. It required also a total transformation of the social substructure – it required health services, education, technical training – in other words it required the creation of an environment in which modern industry could make an impact, and obviously this was something that could not be created overnight.

If one looks at the new states of Asia and Africa one by one, the picture that emerges is not at all uniform. This is not the occasion to examine each country in detail, but there are perhaps a few general patterns which help to illuminate the present situation. We may exclude Japan, which does not really fall into the picture because its history in the last century is totally different from that of any other country in Asia. Japan today seems to stand in the same relation to the newly emancipated countries of Asia as Great Britain did to the countries of continental Europe in 1820. Both, that is to say, stand far ahead – Japan, indeed, is relatively further ahead than Great Britain was in 1820, but the lead can in both cases be called great. In Great Britain's case it was a lead of sixty to seventy years, in the case of Japan I should think not quite so long, simply because things move far more quickly today, but even so probably a lead of between thirty or forty years. Germany in 1820 was still a pre-industrial country, but by 1890 it was catching up on and overtaking Great Britain. Without making predictions, I think it is obvious that China is currently in the midst of a similar process of industrialization and is going to be one of the world's major industrial powers in the course of a generation. Almost certainly its progress will be more rapid than that of the Soviet Union between the first Five Year Plan in 1928 and the present, simply because the tempo of industrialization is so much more rapid today.

But when we turn from China and Japan, which never were really a part of the colonial world (although China was at times near to semi-colonial status), the position is very different. Why is this? There are, of course, a variety of reasons, and I can only suggest a few. First of all, many of the ex-colonial countries, particularly in Africa, are simply too small, both in size and in population – so small that one may reasonably doubt whether, even under the most favourable economic conditions, they can make viable economic units. For example, the Republic of Gabon in tropical Africa has a population roughly equal to a medium-sized American city, but at the same time it has ambassadors and representatives in the United Nations. In other words, it is burdened with the whole topheavy apparatus of a sovereign state without really having the economic substructure to sustain and support it.

Secondly, many of the new states are not really natural units of political and economic life. Particularly in Africa, they represent little more than the administrative divisions which were set up quite artificially for their own purposes by the European colonizing powers after 1880. Often their frontiers cut across tribal and ethnic boundaries. The result is that they are (as social scientists say) 'fissiparous'; that is to say, they are inclined to split up into their constituent parts. That was seen dramatically in Nigeria when the eastern region proclaimed its independence as Biafra in 1967. But Nigeria is only one example, and what is true of Africa is also true of many parts of Asia. Whether Java, Sumatra, the Celebes and the Outer Islands really form one natural political and economic unit is certainly open to question. In any case, it was the Dutch who combined them into one unit, and post-war Indonesia is really the successor of what used to be called before 1939 the Dutch East Indies. Great efforts have been made and are still being made to instil a common sense of Indonesian solidarity, of Indonesian unity and national identity, and it is possible that they will succeed. But the very fact that unity has to be created at this late stage, that it is not a common historical inheritance, is obviously a liability. The history of Pakistan after independence shows only too clearly that unity is not something that can be taken for granted. Not only have the eastern provinces of Pakistan broken off into the separate state of Bangladesh, but there are indications that the four western provinces of Pakistan – the North-West Frontier province, Sind, Punjab and Baluchistan – may also split apart. And, more concealed but unmistakable, there are similar 'fissiparous' tendencies in India. I do not, of course, wish to predict what the future of Pakistan or India will be. All I am saying is that this political instability is a great obstacle to all these countries in their endeavours to carry through a programme of modernization and to secure equal status in fact and not merely in name.

Thirdly, there is political instability of another sort. Often it is the result of an attempt in the first flush of independence to modernize too quickly or to modernize the wrong way, giving priority to the trappings of modernization, to such things as civil airlines, imposing new administrative buildings, etc., instead of building up the economic substructure. This fundamentally was what led to the fall of Kwame Nkrumah in Ghana and which has contributed to the fall of governments and the rise of military dictatorships in country after country since then. The object of statesmen like Nkrumah – in itself, I think, a very sensible object – was to diversify the economy, to make it less dependent on one crop. In the case of Ghana the crop was cocoa. All I will say is that this proved much more difficult in practice than in theory. Whether in fact it is sensible to set up great steel mills which produce steel at a far higher cost than it can be bought on the open market, is an open question. What too often happened, in fact, was that ambitious projects like this proved economically ruinous.

Still, they do point to another of the basic problems which face many of the new countries of Asia and Africa today. This is their dependence on one crop or on one commodity, which of course makes them totally dependent on the world market. It has been calculated, for example, that the fall in the price of coffee by one penny on the New York Commodity Exchange costs the coffee-producing countries of South America 50 million dollars. Much the same is true, for the countries concerned, of tea, tin, rubber and other commodities. This is a basic problem which has not been solved and it leads me to the last of the points which I want to make, namely the tendency for the newly emancipated countries to fall back into dependence on the highly developed industrialized countries of the West. This is the problem which, in some quarters at least, is called neo-colonialism. That was, indeed, the title of one of the last of Kwame Nkrumah's books. Neo-colonialism in simple language means the displacement or replacement of political by economic control through capital investment or in other ways. For example, it is generally accepted that the ex-French colonies of central and equatorial Africa are as closely tied to France today by economic bonds as they were tied by political bonds before emancipation.

These are some of the reasons – there are of course others – why the position of Asia and Africa in the world today, in spite of the remarkable changes which have occurred since 1945, is still in no way commensurate with their size and population. The world is still divided into the rich and the poor – the rich nations which are the developed, industrialized nations, the poor nations which are the underdeveloped nations. Indeed there is no doubt that relatively the rich are getting richer, and the poor are getting poorer; the gap between them, far from narrowing, is growing wider from decade to decade. And it is also true with very few exceptions, of which Japan is obviously the outstanding one, that the rich nations are what are called the white nations and the poor nations the coloured nations.

I think these are perhaps the most important facts in the current world situation; and it is also very important not to misunderstand or misinterpret them. It is possible that the resurgence of Asia and Africa, which has been one of the distinguishing features of the most recent phase of world history, will just peter out, will come to a halt in front of the brick wall of inexorable economic facts. I do not think so myself. First of all, this view leaves out of account the two Asian countries which can turn the balance, namely Japan and China. It assumes that both will throw in their lot with the industrialized countries of the West; and, though I do not want to speculate, I think that over the long run, the next twenty or thirty years, this is unlikely. On the contrary, it seems to me that it will be very important in the world as it is, politically and economically, for Japan and China, in their own interests, to help in the development of the Afro-Asian world.

Secondly, there are steps which the Afro-Asian nations can take to help themselves. If individually, as I have indicated, many of the African states are not viable economic units, the obvious answer is federal union. Admittedly Pan-Africanism has not so far been conspicuously successful as an idea but then, after all, the Pan-European movement, the movement leading to European economic union, to the European Economic Community, also took a long time to get off the ground. And yet it is now a reality, not of course because there were no national differences, national rivalries and jealousies, every bit as serious as those in Africa, but because it was seen to be an economic necessity, a condition of survival. The same can happen in Africa. It is already beginning to happen in Latin America where the problems are similar, and it can happen also in the Middle East. OPEC, the oil exporters' association, although it extends to oil producers outside the Middle East, is perhaps a portent of things to come.

What seems to me certain is that, unless something is done to redress the balance between the West and the rest of the world, unless something is done to make the aspirations of Asians and Africans – which, after all, are not unreasonable or extravagant – into a reality, we are in for trouble. The happiest solution would be for the developed industrial nations, which certainly have benefited over the years from their ability to draw upon the resources of the underdeveloped world, to show in practical terms a sense of their indebtedness, a sense of their duty to help the underdeveloped countries to raise their standard of living. And in fact when UNCTAD, the United Nations Conference on Trade and Development, was first created, there was at least a hope and in many cases an expectation that this would be the case. Unfortunately the third UNCTAD meeting in Santiago, Chile, in the summer of 1972, was like a cold douche, and the fourth UNCTAD meeting in Nairobi in 1976 had no really tangible results. After UNCTAD IV, the prospects of a general joint international effort to right the wrongs, which practically everyone agrees exist, seem to be so small we can almost forget them. As I write, UNCTAD V has just confirmed this unhappy prognostication.

What we cannot forget – what we are not going to be allowed to forget – is the failure, which is a moral as well as an economic failure, of UNCTAD III and UNCTAD IV. Faced by the overwhelming power of the developed nations, the developing countries of Asia and Africa and Latin America have only one alternative, and that is to exploit as best they can the sort of possibilities of threats and intimidation which the petroleum-exporting countries have already used to good effect. Certainly that sort of policy can backfire. The countries who use it may turn out to be the sufferers. But if that sort of confrontation happens, it is going to introduce a poison into relations between the rich, developed nations of the West and the poor, underdeveloped nations of Asia and Africa which will powerfully affect international relations for at least the next generation. Many people would say that it is already doing so.

Unity and cooperation – a challenge for the future

4

In the preceding chapters I have tried to show some of the ways in which the position of Europe, which was the catalyst of the modern world, has changed over the course of time. The resurgence of Asia and Africa evidently reflected a change in the balance of world politics which was the counterpart of the declining position of the European powers – the most active agents in world history in the nineteenth century. Even more important in affecting the situation of Europe in the world was the rise of the two great flanking powers in the East and the West, the Soviet Union, or the Russian empire, as it was until 1917, and the United States. Of course, Russia is historically a European power, but when it expanded into Siberia and Central Asia, it became more than that. The Soviet Union straddles the great Eurasian land mass from the frontiers of Poland in the west right across to Vladivostok on the Pacific coast. And the United States also, although it was colonized by Europeans to a large extent, and although it took over many of its attitudes and ideas from Europe, developed in contradistinction to Europe and also sometimes in rivalry with Europe. So far as it was populated by emigrants from Europe, they were for the most part people who wanted to put memories of Europe behind them and make a new start.

It is unnecessary for our present purposes to trace the historical origins of this great shift in the centres of world civilization and world politics. Certainly they reach back into the nineteenth century. But the decisive factor, quite simply, was the way Europe exhausted itself in the twentieth century in its internal conflicts, in what has been called the great European Civil War. As late as 1913 the United States was a debtor nation. Five years after that, by the end of the First World War, it was the great creditor nation of the world, with the European countries all in its debt. During the first three years of the war, from 1914 to 1917, when the European powers were squandering their resources on fighting each other, the United States built up its industrial potential on a formidable scale. The same was true on a smaller scale of Japan. Engrossed in the European conflict, the European powers had for all practical purposes to ignore the Pacific and the Far East, and therefore the period of the First World War marked a very significant stage in the rise of Japanese industrial and political power.

The position of Russia was different. Although it started from a lower base, in fact from a much lower base, the growth of Russian industry from the 1890s onwards was in relative terms greater than that of any of the European powers, greater than that of Germany, actually greater even than that of the United States. This, together with the size and manpower of Russia, was one of the factors in the German calculations in 1914 – that is to say, the Germans feared that if they did not strike quickly they would be overhauled and overwhelmed by Russia. But Tsarist Russia was a giant with feet of clay. The backwardness of Russian society left it a prey to revolution, and as we all know revolution came first in 1905 and then again in 1917. The revolution of 1917 seemed to eliminate Russia (and in fact for a considerable period actually did eliminate Russia) as a power factor. When, three years later, in 1920 the United States withdrew into isolation, it looked on the surface as though the old position, the pre-1914 world and the pre-war constellation of power, had been restored and that once again Europe was in the saddle.

This, needless to say, was an illusion. As I have said, I do not propose to discuss the origins of the shift in world power away from Europe to the United States and Russia (or rather to the Soviet Union, as after 1917 it had become), but one important feature of the apparent restoration of the position of Europe in the world between 1919 and 1930 is that it was based essentially on the inflow of American capital. In the Pacific the European position was never restored, as was shown clearly enough in 1922 at the Washington Conference. The two powers that really counted in the Pacific after 1922 – the two great naval powers – were Japan and the United States. Elsewhere, an irreversible trend had taken place. Hitler's war, in its broadest significance, can be seen as a last desperate attempt (I say desperate because sometimes I doubt whether even Hitler really believed in the possibility) to fend off the preponderance of the United States and the Soviet Union and to reassert the place of Europe – naturally a Europe under German leadership and German control – in the world. When this attempt failed in 1945, the emergence of a new constellation of world forces was obvious to everyone. Although the British had almost miraculously withstood the German onslaught, the defeat of Hitler was the result first of the terrible sacrifices of the Soviet people and secondly of the immense industrial potential of the United States. The Soviet Union and the United States were the real victors of the war, and the post-war situation reflected this fact.

So much for the history. What arose after 1945, though as I have indicated it had been in preparation a good deal earlier, was a world polarized between the United States and the Soviet Union. Given the circumstances, the result in any case would almost certainly have been rivalry and conflict, even if there had been no ideological differences. But there were basic ideological differences, differences that went back to 1917, differences between Lenin and Wilson, the struggle between Lenin and Wilson to capture the hearts and souls of men, the conflict between the ideal of a socialist organization of society, a society from which the profit motive and private control of the means of production were banished, and, on the other side, a society dedicated to free enterprise, to the free play of economic forces, which most people in the West regarded as the best means of ensuring economic progress. The outcome was the Cold War. We can consider it ideologically as a conflict of capitalism and communism, or we can consider it simply as a conflict of Soviet and American interests, but whichever way one looks at it, it quickly engrossed the whole world.

Unity and cooperation – a challenge for the future

The Cold War shaped and determined the conditions under which we all lived after 1945 and carried with it the ever present threat of a Third World War, a war this time fought with nuclear weapons. Many of us grew up under the shadow of the Cold War and many of us still find it hard to think of it as something in the past. Even today we still have what are called 'cold warriors' with us. They are not all on one side – they can be found in Moscow as well as in Washington – cold warriors preaching an irreconcilable hostility, an inevitable clash between communism and capitalism, between what is called the free world and the communist world. And yet quite clearly things have changed. The situation today is different from what it was in 1947 or 1953, or even in 1957. How far it has changed is another question. When it changed, whether one can put an exact date on the change, whether we can say that in such and such a year the Cold War ended and the world passed on to a new phase, or, if you like, that a new period of world history began, is perhaps an academic question which I do not think need bother us too much. Changes are cumulative, they do not all happen suddenly in one moment. But what is obvious today is that the international situation is not the same as it was in the days when Stalin ruled Russia and when John Foster Dulles presided over United States foreign policy as Secretary of State.

How did this great change come about? For ten years at least after the end of the Second World War, it looked as if the two great superpowers were forcing the whole world into two monolithic blocs. In fact, to be neutral, to try to stand aside, was regarded almost as treason. But even then it was evident that this polarization of the world could not and would not last forever. In both camps, the American and the Russian, in the capitalist as in the communist camp, the satellites chafed at their subordination, chafed at the subjection of their interests to the interests or alleged interests in one case of Moscow, in the other of Washington. In Asia and Africa, there was growing resistance to being forced to take sides in a struggle which many Asians and many Africans regarded as a quarrel between two branches of the white world and really none of their business. That was the position formulated by Nehru of India and by Nasser of Egypt at the Bandung Conference in 1955. Though its immediate practical results may not have been particularly significant, Bandung symbolized a reaction against the Cold War mentality, and for that reason 1955 may be looked on as a symbolic date.

It is a symbolic date also because by that time, indeed at that very time, there were signs of a similar shift of thinking in Europe, on both sides of the so-called Iron Curtain. In Eastern Europe, events after the death of Stalin in 1953, events which culminated at the time of the 20th Party Congress of the Soviet Union in 1956, showed at least that in the communist camp the situation was less monolithic than it had been, that the communist or socialist countries of Eastern Europe had at any rate greater liberty to conduct their own affairs. A certain recognition was given (we may debate how much, but it is a fact that it was given) to what was called 'national communism', that is, the right of the different communist countries to follow their own road to socialism. And in Western Europe at the same time there were plenty of signs of change. By 1955 the developments which led to the formation of the European Economic Community were already far advanced, though the Treaty of Rome, which formally constituted the European Economic Community, was not actually signed until 1957. And though of course there were many other factors which contributed to the movement for European unity, there is no doubt that anti-Americanism, in the sense of determination to resist dictation from Washington, to strengthen Europe so it could take an independent course, was one of them, particularly on the part of De Gaulle.

Thus around 1955 we see the first signs of a new constellation of forces. They should not be exaggerated, but it is evident in retrospect that they marked the slow beginning of a realignment which has come to fruition in our own day. The next stage, perhaps the decisive stage, was the much discussed Sino-Soviet conflict. I suspect its practical consequences may have been overstated, but it did indicate at least two things. First, it revealed a marked difference between China and the Soviet Union as to the tactics which the communist powers should pursue in the present constellation of world affairs, and this in fact reflected two different and conflicting interpretations of Marxism. Secondly, it revealed a rivalry between Soviet Russia and China for leadership of the communist camp.

The Sino-Soviet conflict also had a marked effect on United States policy. In the years immediately after 1945 the enemy for the United States was the Soviet Union. American policy was directed quite openly towards what was called 'containing' Soviet expansion. In the second stage – perhaps it began with the Korean War, perhaps it did not come until later – the United States saw Communist China as the main enemy. Whether that was a correct calculation is another question. In retrospect, it looks to have been mistaken. So far as the evidence goes, it is pretty clear that the Vietnamese nationalists received more support from the Soviet Union than from the Chinese People's Republic. It is also well known that the Vietnamese are suspicious historically of China's inclination to regard Vietnam as a sort of client state – a suspicion that came out into the open following the end of the Vietnamese war and the reunification of Vietnam. Nevertheless, when from the time of John F. Kennedy the United States got bogged down more and more in Vietnam, it came to see China rather than the Soviet Union as its chief opponent and there was a growing tendency in Washington to try to play off Moscow against Peking. Particularly after the dismissal of Khrushchev and his replacement by Kosygin and Brezhnev, the Soviet Union was seen as a satiated power with an interest in the status quo, as a country which had made the transition to industrialization and now wanted to enjoy the benefits of it in peace, and which therefore had interests in common with the United States. The symbol of this was the famous 'hot line' between the White House and the Kremlin, the direct line of communication which would enable the two superpowers to settle their differences directly over the heads of their allies and associates. All this indicated that the pattern of international relations was changing, that the Cold War, at any rate the Cold War as it was interpreted around 1950, was a thing of the past.

But more fundamental than any of this, though less discussed, was the sheer cost of the Cold War. We know for obvious reasons more about the American than the Russian side, but on both sides there is no doubt that the cost in the long run was prohibitive. Nuclear weapons, stockpiling of H bombs, space programmes, intercontinental ballistic missiles and anti-missiles and anti-missile defensive systems, this whole paraphernalia of Cold War imposed a huge burden, so huge in fact that only the two great superpowers could undertake it and second-class powers like Great Britain simply had to withdraw from the race. At first the United States, confident in what Dean Acheson called its 'unlimited creative capacity', embarked happily on this immense programme and the President was officially advised in 1950 that the United States could indefinitely devote 20 per cent of its gross national product to armaments without in any way endangering economic stability. Of course it was a gross miscalculation. But when in addition, as happened from around 1955, both the two superpowers began to compete in giving economic aid, which in reality meant buying or trying to buy allies, another factor entered. And finally, on top of all this, there was the mounting American involvement in Vietnam, the build-up of forces until in the end over half a million ground troops were involved. This was the factor that tipped the scales. By 1968 it was obvious that the United States was over-extended. In fact, 9 per cent of its gross national product and over 50 per cent of government expenditure was going on the military establishment. The year 1968 proved to be the turning point. Among the reasons why President Nixon was elected, certainly one of the most important, was the desire to cut back the commitment in Vietnam, to withdraw ground troops, to restore economic equilibrium and to devote more attention to the internal requirements of the country.

About the Soviet Union we are much less well informed in detail, but there is no doubt that the strains imposed by the Cold War on the Soviet Union must have been even greater. The Soviet Union, after all, started with an economy suffering from war devastation. It started from a very much lower base. It had to build its armaments industry – that is to say, its nuclear armaments industry – at top speed, and that necessitated for years a gross imbalance in the Soviet economy. It meant the sacrifice of the interests of the consumers, of consumer goods for the Russian people and even of such basic necessities as housing, to the alleged military necessities. Moreover, a similar regime of austerity was imposed also on the countries of Eastern Europe and naturally this caused a lot of discontent and a lot of anti-Russian feeling. All one needs to say is that the Soviet Government must have felt far more than the American administration in Washington the need for relaxation, the need for a détente, for some way out of the Cold War.

That is the background to the changes in the international situation which came about swiftly after 1968 and which reached a peak, so far as we can judge, in 1972 and 1973. These changes are still so near to us, their ramifications are still so uncertain, that one is a little hesitant about trying to draw conclusions or to analyse their implications. But I think one thing is clear – that we all feel we have entered into a new period of history. The specific concrete results are perhaps not yet fully evident, and there are threats from time to time, particularly since the accession to power of the Carter administration in the United States, that the attitudes and mentality of the Cold War may be revived. But there is no doubt that the chain of events beginning with President Nixon's journeys to Moscow and Peking changed the climate of international relations. In particular, United States recognition of the Chinese People's Republic and, following its recognition, the entry of China into the United Nations created a new situation. The refusal to recognize the consequences of the Chinese Revolution of 1949, like the refusal after the First World War to recognize the consequences of the Russian Revolution of 1917, was the great anomaly and in many ways the underlying weakness of the old international system. You cannot build a stable international order by ignoring and ostracizing one of the world's largest and most populous countries.

That does not mean, of course, that the entry of China into the United Nations suddenly brought a new stability into international relations. Also, we must not make the mistake of dramatizing or over-dramatizing Nixon's initiatives and the new relations between Washington and Moscow and Washington and Peking. There was certainly a tendency to do so at the time. But such events, although they may symbolize or even highlight the change, do not themselves create a new situation. The real changes went much deeper. For twenty years after 1945, the United States was the dominant power because it emerged from the war with the strongest industrial base, a vast capital accumulation and a vast gold reserve. The recovery of Europe and the recovery of Japan were only possible through American aid, which was given on a lavish scale. But around 1963 the situation began to change. European and Japanese industry became more competitive and at the same time American industry became less competitive. And so a period of dollar shortage, what was called 'the dollar gap', gave way to a period of dollar surplus. The details are technical and complicated and I will not go into them. The simple fact is that, as the United States deficit in its balance of payments grew to something like 11 billion dollars, the 'dollar era' came to an end; and by the beginning of the 1970s, the United States was in the throes of a deep-seated crisis. It was not merely an economic but also a spiritual crisis, and it shook America's self-confidence and its claim to be the leader of the free world. The result was that a world divided into two blocs was succeeded, though the outlines are still far from clear, by the beginnings of a new balance of power, which looks, this time, as though it will be regional rather than national.

That, very briefly, is the economic background of the great change in the pattern of international relations which has occurred in the last few years. Once again we must not make the mistake of dramatizing or exaggerating it. The essential interests of the United States and of the Soviet Union and China have not changed; all that has changed is the way they think it is best to maintain and defend them. None of the three great powers is likely to retreat from its long-term objectives. What we must envisage rather is a stabilization of the existing frontiers between the power blocs, a maintenance of positions which have been won and which, if they can, they are all going to hold.

The United States certainly has given up the idea which was so popular in Mr Dulles' day of throwing back communism, but neither side is likely to allow changes in the present balance which are plainly to its disadvantage. It is true that Vietnam has been reunited; but it seems unlikely that Korea will be reunited in the foreseeable future, in spite of initiatives in both North Korea and South Korea for some sort of reunification, any more than in Europe the two Germanies are likely to be reunited. As a matter of fact, one of the first signs of the emergence of a new situation was the dropping of the cry for German reunification which was so insistent for the first twenty years after the Second World War, and the recognition by Germans in both halves of Germany of the independent existence of the two German Republics. In the Middle East also, it is highly unlikely that either Russia or the United States will allow, or that either of them will attempt, any fundamental change in the existing balance. The Soviet Union will support Syria if Israel seems to be getting too strong, and the United States will certainly prevent any Arab plan to wipe Israel from the map. But it will also not underwrite – and perhaps will actively oppose – Israeli expansionism.

What seems to be emerging, in place of the polarized world of the first twenty years after the Second World War, is a world of great regional blocs, a system of regions of which (as far as we can see today) the main ones will be the Soviet bloc, North America, the Arab world of North Africa and the Middle East, China, Western Europe, South or Latin America (including Mexico), and sub-Saharan Africa. This leaves some anomalies. What, for example, is the position of Japan going to be in this new regional world? There are also other important countries and areas which I have not mentioned – for one, Australia, which I think is likely, like Canada, to gravitate into the North American orbit, though probably in neither case very willingly. Then there are areas like Southeast Asia whose future is very unclear. Will South-east Asia form another regional unit in a regional world, or is it going to remain divided as it has been divided in the last twenty years between the influence of Russian and Chinese and American imperialism? Even after the withdrawal from Vietnam I cannot easily foresee the United States withdrawing entirely from South-east Asia because it regards it, rightly or wrongly, as a necessary strategic outpost in its defensive system. But the situation can and almost certainly will change in the course of time.

We must remember that this new pattern is still tentative and fluid; it is more a possibility than a reality. It is also a very imperfect response to the real needs of world society today. We should regard it more as a pragmatic reaction to changing conditions than as an ideal structure of international organization. One major defect is that it does little justice to the legitimate desires of small peoples – and south Asia in particular is full of small peoples, such as the Karens, the Shans, the Kachins, the Nagas – for independence and for a national life of their own. On the other hand, the new regionalism has a certain logic behind it. The development of science and technology, the sheer scale of modern industry, have made the national unit in many respects an anachronism in the modern world, particularly as there are now almost twice as many national states as there were before the Second World War. For example, English, French, German computer industries all competing for a market which is already too small does not make sense; but a single West European computer industry does. Economies of scale, rationalization of production, call today for a regional system. That every country of Africa, every country of Eastern Europe, every country of Latin America, should seek to have its own airline, its own steel production, its own automobile industry, is irrational and self-defeating. That is why the idea of a South American Common Market, a Pan-African Federation, or in Eastern Europe the idea behind COMECON, the Council for Mutual Economic Assistance, fits into contemporary patterns. Of course the obstacles to regional associations, particularly those on the political level, are immense, but so are the advantages; and I think that slowly, and no doubt with many setbacks, these regional organizations will crystallize simply because not to have them would spell disaster.

The model for regional organization is the enlarged European Common Market, the European Economic Community. Its basic purpose has been to restore Europe, by eliminating national frontiers, to the place it had in the world before 1914, to make it competitive in a world of great regional blocs with the United States and the Soviet Union. Whether it will succeed is another question. Restoration is easier said than done and recent quarrels over a common agricultural policy and over monetary union reveal some of the problems and obstacles. But the decisive question about the European Economic Community for the rest of the world is a different one. It is the question whether it is going to be an inward-looking or an outward-looking community. If it erects tariff barriers, if it forms itself into a tight, closed trading bloc and cuts itself off from the rest of the world as far as it can–and there are plenty of signs that this is what may happen – it will be a bad and dangerous precedent for the rest of the world.

Unity and cooperation – a challenge for the future

Back in the 1930s, under the pressure of economic stringency caused by the great depression, the world experienced a period of restrictive trade policies, of trading blocs and of separate monetary areas (the sterling area, the dollar area, the yen area, and others). The result was the growth of rivalries which ultimately found their outlet in war. No doubt the economic crises we have experienced since 1970 – the crisis of 1970–72 and again of 1974 and 1975 – were very different from the economic crisis of 1930 to 1932. Even so, it would be foolish to ignore the danger that the rise of regional blocs may reproduce the same sort of situation, but this time on a larger scale. For example, there has been much talk of a revival of isolationism in the United States; that is to say, of the possibility of the United States turning its back on the world, concentrating on its own immense internal market, shutting out external competition. Though it was only a temporary measure, President Nixon's imposition in August 1971 of the 10 per cent surcharge on imports was a foretaste of what might happen. Since then there have been pressures on Japan more than once to restrict its exports under threat of the imposition of quotas. Whether such measures, increasingly frequent in the last few years, will become the rule, is impossible to say. The outcome in all probability will depend upon the attitudes of other countries, particularly of the European countries, to the United States' trading and balance of payments problems, and so far they have not been very understanding or very helpful.

The implications of this situation are particularly serious for countries which do not fit neatly into the new regional pattern. Among these, Japan is probably the most outstanding. I have already asked what Japan's place will be in the new regional world which appears to be emerging. There is no doubt that President Nixon's change of policy, particularly towards China, created an uncomfortable situation for Japan. It was only to be expected that Prime Minister Tanaka would draw the logical conclusion and try to put Sino-Japanese relations on a new and more cooperative basis. But the new initiative towards China, although it opened up new possibilities for Japan, still left the basic questions unanswered. Among these none is more important than the question of the relations of Japan as one of the world's greatest industrial nations to the highly developed industrialized countries of the West, the United States and the European community, on the one hand, and its relations with the underdeveloped world of Asia on the other hand. Where, in short, does Japan's future lie? With Asia, with the West, or with both?

No one, I think, can answer that question at this stage, but it is certainly one of the big questions of the future, not only for Japan but for the whole world. The major problem facing the world in the last quarter of the twentieth century is the problem of under-development, and there is a real danger of the world drawing apart into two blocs once again, but this time with the wealthy, in-dustrialized countries on one side and the poorer underdeveloped countries of Asia and Africa on the other side. Where does Japan stand in this? It is exceptional among Asian countries because it is a rich country, but can it afford to ignore its traditional links with its neighbours in Asia and throw in its lot with the West? Will it not compromise itself in Asian eyes if it sides with the rich white countries? Much will depend upon the answers Japan gives to these questions. No other country, perhaps, is better placed to take the lead.

When I look back over what I have tried to say in these pages it seems to me that there are a few simple lessons. The first is that in a world which science and technology have made one, we simply cannot afford to fall back into regional isolation. We are all in the same boat, and a state of poverty, backwardness, underdevelop-ment in one part of the world is bound to react on all of us. Secondly, we cannot afford the luxury of ideologies and ideologi-cal conflicts. To that degree the relaxation of tension between Washington and Moscow and Washington and Peking is certainly a good thing provided – but only provided – that we do not allow the old conflict between communism and capitalism to be suc-ceeded by a new ideological conflict between the developed and the underdeveloped worlds, between the rich and the poor, which might too easily develop into a race war. The third thing is the pervasiveness of imperialism, which may change its form but does not change its reality. The European imperial powers withdrew from political empire after 1947, but their economic power still gives them leverage in the world, just as economic power gives leverage to the United States. The world is not made up of equal peoples. In fact, in many important ways, inequalities are increasing rather than decreasing. There are still the industrialized countries at the centre and the underdeveloped countries on the periphery. What we need is a world without centre and periphery, a world of equal peoples. Despite the tremendous contribution of the West in the sustained growth of science and technology, a growth which, as we have seen, is transforming the face of the world, there can be no centre and no periphery in world history for any length of time, and any attempt to maintain that division can only result in conflict. In the long run, salvation is the result of recognizing the fundamental unity of mankind, the fact that, in spite of different social organizations, different values, different cultural traditions, everywhere there are basic similarities of human nature, human thinking and human responses. To recognize that seems to me the challenge of the twenty-first century, a challenge to build an international order based on equality, not on power, based on cooperation, not on conflict, based on reason, not on fear. It would be optimistic to suppose we can achieve it; but if we fail, the future we shall leave to our children scarcely bears thinking about.

Culture and civilization

5

The story I have told in the preceding pages leaves us with some unsettling questions. We have seen how a civilization which originated in Europe succeeded, through its scientific and technological proficiency, in imposing its image on the world. The question is: at what cost? The march of science may be irreversible; it does not follow that it solves all the questions. Some people might say that it creates more problems than it solves. If it is true, on one level, that science and technology have made the whole world one, in the sense that scientific discovery cannot be imprisoned within national boundaries, it is also true, on another level, that the rise of a single world civilization has produced a sense of alienation and a revulsion against uniformity. It has raised the old question of civilization and culture – the question whether the march of civilization is compatible with the preservation of cultural values, and whether we lose more than we gain if we squander our cultural heritage.

What this means is that the postulates which lie at the heart of modern industrial society are being questioned on a number of different fronts and at a number of different levels. The first casualty, perhaps, is the happy confidence, so characteristic of the generation after 1945, that the achievements of modern science have given us the technical knowledge and managerial skills to solve any problem and surmount any crisis. Instead, it begins to look as though science has put us on a pedestal from which, sooner or later, we are going to topple. According to a poll taken in 1973, more than 60 per cent of Americans had lost faith in the ability of government 'to solve problems'. If they had, how much more so must that be true of other less pragmatical peoples.

Secondly, there are doubts about the viability over the long run – perhaps even over the short run – of the sort of society we have created for ourselves. From its very inception modern industrial society has been expansive; ever-increasing productivity has been its life-blood. The famous economist and Nobel prize-winner, Wassily Leontief, has calculated that, if we continue at the present rate with no acceleration, we shall use up between three and four times as much of the world's mineral resources during the remainder of the twentieth century as were consumed during the entire previous history of civilization. The unanswered question today is how long this squandering of irreplaceable resources can go on unchecked, and what in any event is the future of a civilization whose very basis is ceaseless growth and conspicuous consumption.

These are questions which have been touched on in earlier sections of this book, and I do not propose to discuss them further. They account, in part at least, for the growing doubt whether the promise of industrial society will be – and, indeed, whether realistically it can be – matched by performance. They explain why what used to be called the 'revolution of rising expectations' has turned into a 'revolution of rising frustrations'. According to the distinguished Cambridge scientist, Peter Medawar, 'the goal of a happy, high-consumption world cannot be fulfilled even for the 3.5 billion people now alive, much less the 6 billion expected by the year 2000. At the American standard of living, the earth could support only 500 million.' If that is the case, it would seem that the time has come to think again.

But there is another question which is perhaps even more insistent, and that is whether the sort of future industrial society promises – whether or not it can produce it – is really the sort of future we want. It is possible, in other words, that under the impact of Western science and Western technology the world took off in a wrong direction; and the fact that, to all appearances, continuous expansion and ever-increasing productivity are unsustainable objectives – the fact that to all appearances we are rapidly approaching the end of a road – gives the question an actuality, and an urgency, it did not possess a generation ago. If, on the one side, there is a disenchantment with the products of industrial society and a fear that it may be leading us into a blind alley, on the other side there is a growing perception that the advance of civilization is destroying, or at least is engulfing, inherited cultural values.

It is no accident that the dichotomy between modern technological civilization and traditional cultural values is felt most strongly in Asia and Africa. In the West, modern society grew by fairly regular stages out of traditional society; there were many uncomfortable moments, but there was no sudden break, no direct confrontation. In Asia and Africa the West forced its values, often at gunpoint, on peoples who had no desire to adopt them. Neither China nor Japan wished to open its ports to the West. The Chinese proudly told George III's ambassadors that there was nothing they needed from the Western barbarians. And although China, as Joseph Needham has shown, was ahead of Europe – sometimes millennia ahead – in basic scientific discoveries, it did not exploit them to enforce its dominance or impose its cultural values; it did not, for instance, think of gunpowder, as Europeans did, as a means of destroying its enemies. The famous Italian Jesuit, Matteo Ricci, who lived in China between 1582 and 1610, was quick to perceive the essential difference. 'The nations of the West,' he wrote, 'seem to be entirely consumed with the idea of supreme domination'; whereas in China, 'though they have a well-equipped army and navy that could easily conquer the neighbouring nations, neither the ruler nor his people ever think of waging a war of aggression.'

This attitude, deeply rooted in Confucian values, contrasts strikingly with the forceful spirit of Western society. It made China vulnerable to Western material superiority, but it did not imply cultural or spiritual inferiority, and the Chinese were always aware of the difference. When the British fought their way up the Canton River in 1841, the Cantonese denounced them for seeking profit like animals seeking food. 'Except for your ships being solid, your gunfire fierce, and your rockets powerful, what good qualities do you have?' And eighty years later, after the First World War, the Chinese writer Yen Fu summed up what he called 'the three centuries of progress' in the West under four headings: 'to be selfish, to kill others, to have no integrity, and to lose the sense of shame.' That is how the accomplishments of Western civilization appeared to an observer from outside.

Historians have discussed at length the sources of the thrusting, restless dynamism of the West. They have been traced to the impact of Cartesian philosophy, with its belief in the powers of human reason to solve the mysteries of the universe, and to the proselytizing zeal and militancy of the Christian religion, so different from the otherworldliness of Buddhism and Hinduism and the equipoise of Confucianism. The question of origins is not perhaps important in the present context. What is important is that a religious fanaticism, which seems to have developed in Europe in the course of the eleventh century, was transformed later into a secular religion, the religion of success. And from this secular religion, which later took root in New England, spring both the overweening confidence in man's ability to solve his problems by his own unaided skills and the thrustfulness of the new industrial society. They reflect a peculiarly Western attitude to the world.

At one time Westerners took pride in it; they spoke, with a sense of superiority, of the 'Faustian spirit' of Western society. Some still do; but the number of dissentient voices is growing. The reason, in part, is disillusion with the religion of success, a realization of the emptiness – almost the pointlessness – of growth and affluence as ends in themselves. But there is also increasing awareness that the onward march of civilization destroys as much as it creates. Paradoxically, the world we have created for ourselves, in spite of its amenities, is a place few people – even the apparently favoured 'jet set' – find satisfying; and so they dash, those who can afford it, from New York to Monte Carlo to Paris to Honolulu to the Bahamas in search of a satisfaction which eludes them. For the bulk of mankind, on the other hand, for the teeming millions in factories and offices, life is a more or less dull routine, relieved (if they are lucky) by what the Romans called *panis et circenses* – in modern terms, by the Saturday afternoon football game and

79

weekend drinking, beer for the poor and whisky for the more affluent. And with this goes the realization that culture and civilization are not the same thing – that you can be civilized but not cultured, and cultured but not civilized.

The dichotomy between civilization and culture was the central preoccupation of Oswald Spengler, one of the great though currently unpopular and neglected thinkers of our century. For Spengler the history of mankind is, in essence, the story of the supersession of culture by a thin layer of civilization imposed, usually, by a predatory, expanding imperialism – a layer so thin that eventually it cracks and the cycle begins anew. This is the theme of Spengler's *Decline of the West*, and subsequently Arnold Toynbee, who took up where Spengler left off, showed how the fabric of civilization was torn apart, time after time, by the combined assault of an internal and external proletariat, both deprived of their cultural heritage and alienated from the dominant civilization and its values. If we look closely enough, I think, something of the sort is visible on the contemporary horizon.

Culture, in the sense in which Spengler and Toynbee used the word, is the antithesis of civilization. It is the product of long tradition, of shared habits among people living together over generations; it reflects a particular way of life and a particular view of the world. Its characteristic is spontaneity, and it is often said that it cannot be exported or imported. Civilization, by contrast, is mechanistic. It provides the mechanism and the ideology necessary to hold together large-scale political societies, and this today implies high technological requirements (without which the whole body politic might collapse); but in most essentials the mechanism was little different in earlier times in simpler but extensive empires like Babylon or Persia or the Han empire of China. These also were underpinned not only by an apparatus of government but also by a set of values imposed on the subject peoples, sometimes by force but more often by persuasion and example.

In practice, of course, the distinction between civilization and culture was never as clear-cut as these definitions suggest. It is not true, for example, that culture cannot be exported. Much of the history of China – certainly of early China under the Ch'in and Han dynasties – is the story of the assimilation of more primitive peoples, particularly in the south, into the prevalent Chinese culture. Culture is something created, not given. Even in the British Isles, which, like Japan, seem predestined by their insularity to form a single cultural entity, its formation was a long and slow process, and Scotland and Wales were never fully assimilated. But even in England itself, as we know from *The Paston Letters*, the very language, to say nothing of the customs, of Englishmen north of the Trent was so different in the fifteenth century from that of Londoners that they probably had difficulty in understanding each other. If England is a cultural unity today, it is certainly one that has existed only in very recent times. When Elizabeth Gaskell published her outstanding novel *North and South* in 1855, she was writing of two distinct cultures or ways of life. Paradoxically, it seems, it was the railways, linking London and Manchester in four or five hours and reducing the ancient city of York, up to that time the capital of the north, to the status of a provincial town, that created the cultural unity we call England.

What this suggests is that the relations of culture and civilization are more complex than appears at first glance to be the case, that technological advance affects not only the material structure of life but also the cultural environment. Culture is always in flux. When the famous Japanese writer and artist Yukio Mishima committed hara kiri in 1970, his action was regarded in Japan not as a recall to ancient virtues, but as an anachronism. It was part of a cultural tradition that had died. Furthermore, we should resist the temptation, to which many intellectuals are prone, of extolling culture at the expense of civilization. Culture also has its dark sides. When the English condemned the practice of suttee, or widow-burning, in nineteenth-century India, they were attacked for interfering with Indian tradition; but it is hard to think that any Indian today would say that they were wrong. That is why it is important to insist that, in spite of different cultural traditions, there are basic human values to which we must adhere if we wish to maintain civilized standards of living.

And, of course, we *do* wish to maintain civilized standards of living – just as those, still the vast majority of mankind, who have never enjoyed them, wish to attain them. The amenities of civilization cannot be lightly fobbed off. I personally would be sorry to be writing these words by candlelight, as the Duke of Wellington wrote his despatches in a drafty tent during the Napoleonic wars. Still less would I like to have to get up at dawn or before dawn – though that is what millions of people still have to do – to light a fire and heat the water before my hands are warm enough to pick up my pen. In any case, there is no going back. Whatever the West has done to the East – and in some respects (for example, the improved position of women) it would be hard to show that it was detrimental – it has become a fact of life. Japan, whether we like it or not, is going to continue to be a manufacturer and exporter of Datsuns and Toyotas, and this is bound to affect, and has already dramatically affected, the tone and character of Japanese life, just as it is bound to affect the other countries which are emulating, with greater or lesser success, the Japanese example. The complexity of industrial society simply does not permit the relatively simple techniques and standards by which earlier predominantly agrarian societies were regulated.

If this is anywhere near the truth, then it would seem that the essential problem facing us today is how to reconcile the preservation of the cultural differences all people feel and most people cherish – differences reflecting centuries or millennia of shared historical experience – with the need, which we all know exists, though we may resent and resist it, to organize the world, with its limited and irreplaceable resources, in such a way that we can survive into the twenty-first century. It is a problem I am far from convinced we are capable of resolving. The great civilizations have always been, in Eric Voegelin's expressive phrase, 'a graveyard of societies' – in other words, expansionist and submerging smaller, indigenous cultures in their expansion. This is true from the time of the Medes and Persians, whose ruler Cyrus the Great proudly proclaimed himself 'king of the four quarters of the world', down to the present. The Greeks assumed that their world was the equivalent of the *oikoumene*, the Romans that the *orbis terrarum* was coextensive with the jurisdiction of Rome, the Chinese that the Middle Kingdom was the centre of the universe, the sole repository of civilization. Similarly the British in the nineteenth century saw their dominions as 'the empire on which the sun never sets' and spoke scornfully of 'the lesser tribes without the law'. The dominant people were 'the lords of mankind'; the rest were 'barbarians' or 'natives'.

In part, no doubt, this attitude is racialist, but only in part. It springs also from the self-assurance of a successful, expanding civilization, convinced that its values are superior to any others, or even that they represent eternal verities. Two thousand years ago the Romans propagated and exported the Roman way of life; similarly today Americans propagate the American way of life. The result is a kind of cultural colonialism, more insidious perhaps than sheer predatory colonialism, and no better because it is often motivated by benevolence and a genuine sense of mission. Incredibly, General Westmoreland believed he was conferring a boon on the Vietnamese when, having demolished their cities and temples and devastated their countryside, he provided them with eight airfields, 11 million square feet of covered storage space and 2.5 million cubic feet of cold storage. 'In a short time,' he wrote, 'South Vietnam acquired facilities possessed by few nations other than the most highly developed.' What it lost, he does not say and appears not even to comprehend.

For the Vietnamese and other peoples involved – for the victims of progress, or at least its unconsulted objects – the position is almost directly the reverse. What they see is the way their inherited culture is being engulfed and destroyed by the spreading tentacles of a uniform, standardized civilization, underpinned by values and assumptions they do not share. The islands of the Pacific and the Caribbean are being turned into a Western playground, their peoples into the helots of the affluent West – servants, porters, kitchen hands, guides, attendants. No wonder the West Indian poet Aimé Césaire declaims against the white world and praises 'those who never invented anything' and 'those who never conquered anything'.

Not surprisingly, this perception is strong among the peoples on the periphery of the self-styled civilized world. But it is not confined to them. One of the significant developments of the last quarter of a century is the reassertion by peoples living in the very heart of advanced Western countries – what are sometimes patronizingly called the 'subcultures' – of their individuality and of their right to lead their own lives as they think best. In France,

Bretons, Corsicans, Alsatians and the Occitanians of Gascony and Provence are struggling to free themselves from the heavy hand of Paris; in Spain, Basques and Catalans are resisting subordination to Castile. Belgium is divided between Flemings and Walloons, and in the British Isles Wales and Scotland, which everyone fifty years ago regarded as integral parts of a single United Kingdom, are demanding some form of autonomy. With these instances before our eyes, there is no need to turn to the desperate Kurdish resistance to Iraq, or the long struggle of the Nagas for independence from India, to see that cultural differences are a major fact in a world which is technologically becoming one.

It is true that other factors are involved besides cultural differences and a determination to salvage ancient cultures submerged by the advance of the centralizing nation state. The revolt against technocratic society is taking place simultaneously on a number of different fronts. Many of the peoples involved in the revolt inhabit regions handicapped on an economic as well as on a cultural level, and their demand for autonomy is directed, at least in part, against economic subordination to the interests of the dominant ethnic group. In this sense we can speak of a rebellion of the internal proletariat, an uprising of the underprivileged regions. At the same time we are witnessing a revolt against the frustration, anonymity and sheer mechanical tedium of life in the factory and on the shop-floor, and against the dehumanizing consequences of large-scale industry. In other words, the more the spread of industrial society enforces a convergence of life-styles, the more the peoples of the world are insisting on their autonomy and individuality. This is the paradox at the heart of contemporary industrial society, and it goes far to explain the crisis of modern industrial civilization.

What we are discovering, slowly and belatedly, is that it is easy to impose a civilization but difficult to depose a culture. And yet this has always been the case. The history of Persia is essentially the story of the survival of Persian culture under successive layers of Greek, Roman, Arab and Turkish civilization, and only the other day we have seen how Persian traditionalists are ready to fight to defend their cultural identity against the Shah's 'modernizing' policies. In the West, archaeologists have shown how Celtic forms of art survived through four centuries of Roman imperial rule and quickly came to the surface again after the Roman legions were withdrawn. It would be easy to cite other examples, but it is not necessary. The simple fact is that the strength of tradition and the weakness of civilization is, in the end, a question of numbers. India was the heart of the British empire; but even at the height of British imperial power there were only some 300,000 British in Asia in an aggregate population of over 300 millions. The same is true of the other great imperial powers of history. Spread thinly over a vast territorial expanse, they could only keep their empire in being with the aid of the subject peoples; when this was denied or withdrawn the day of reckoning was near.

I am not suggesting, of course, that the diffusion of civilization is simply a question of force and power. When, at the very beginning of the present century, the well-known English journalist W. T. Stead wrote his influential tract, *The Americanization of the World*, he was not thinking of the imposition of the American way of life by force of arms, but of the way American ideas and American practices were permeating the rest of the world by a process of peaceful penetration. It looked for long as though he was right, as though the world was being Americanized. Today it is not so certain. Even in the United States itself the mythology of the American way of life is being questioned, and the old picture of America as a 'melting pot' is ceasing to be true. Generations of immigrants asked nothing better than to forget their past and submerge their cultural differences in a common American life-style, and the primary aim of American education was to mould them and their children in a single pattern. Today this is no longer the case. The Black movement is directed quite specifically against assimilation. Chicanos and Puerto Ricans do not wish to be absorbed. On the contrary, they assert their Hispanic cultural background against the dominant Anglo-Saxon one and demand Spanish-speaking schools, just as the Cajuns of Louisiana – like the Québecois in Canada – cling to the French language and to their inherited cultural traditions. The melting pot, once so potent an attraction, has lost its potency.

These are facts we should remember when we are told that the 'ultimate convergence of life-styles' is 'inevitable'. The mere fact that people dress alike – that jeans, originally the garb of the

American West, are the preferred garment of young people, male and female, from Warsaw to Osaka – or that pop music has adherents everywhere, in Moscow and Paris as much as in San Francisco or New York, can be interpreted as a sign of cultural convergence; but it is convergence of a very superficial kind. Reinforced concrete and high-rise buildings may be ubiquitous; but Rome, Paris, Boston, Rio de Janeiro, each has its own distinctive architectural style. The prevalence of the film as a world-wide form of popular entertainment is often cited as evidence of a growing homogeneity of civilization. But a Japanese film, or an English or French or Italian film, is quite different from an American film; they reflect the cultural differences of the producers and actors, and no one could possibly confuse them.

Cultural traditions have deep roots – far deeper, usually, than the civilization grafted on to them. That is why it is rarely possible to impose the patterns of one society on another for any length of time. The failure of cultural assimilation is a theme running through history. It was the experience of the Greek colonies of Asia Minor in classical times, and of the Latin states of Syria in the Middle Ages. It has been seen more recently in the fate of British parliamentary institutions in the former British colonies, and there is no reason to think that the process is at an end. Not, of course, that any people anywhere is going deliberately to turn its back on modern science and technology, even if it could. But that does not mean that they are ready to see their cultural identity submerged and lost under a veneer of technocratic civilization. For a time it looked as though they would. For a century people scrambled eagerly for the amenities of civilization – electricity, the motor car, central heating, refrigerators, and the rest – and for the style of life they made possible. It looks now as though we have reached a turning point. Today it is technocratic civilization that is under assault, both from within and from without. Fewer and fewer people regard it as the desired goal, fewer and fewer people share the illusion of its permanence. And more and more people are beginning to wonder whether its onward march, if it continues as it has done during the past quarter of a century, is not a recipe for disaster.

The conclusion I would draw is that it is time to think again about the future of Western civilization, or at least about the direction in which it is going. A great deal has been written in recent years – most of it distinctly pessimistic – about the dangers ahead and the possibility of imminent disaster. It is a characteristic sign of the current cultural malaise, and shows at least a growing awareness of the fragility and precariousness of civilization. But it is a one-sided literature, preoccupied almost exclusively with the symptoms of material breakdown and scarcely at all with the possibility of cultural breakdown. Few of the writers seem to be aware of the groundswell which is shaking technological civilization at its foundations. Most simply assume that the sort of society in which we live – modified, of course, and adapted to enable it to survive in an age of scarcity and burgeoning population – will continue to set the pattern of the future. Most assume also that 'modernization' – by which they mean the diffusion of Western values, Western technology, Western political ideas and Western institutions – is the only practicable way forward. Neither proposition is as self-evident as its proponents believe. Admittedly, the evidence is bound to be inconclusive at the present stage of a transformation which is just beginning. But the trend, so far as we can see, appears to be in the opposite direction – towards political decentralization and economic decentralization, towards a rejection of the domination of the great metropolitan centres and transnational structures and a reassertion of cultural traditions and cultural autonomy. Everywhere, if we look around, we can see the symptoms of profound social and political change – peoples reclaiming their past and striving to reconquer it, and states and empires faltering and unable to cope with the problems besetting them. This is the classic setting for a restructuring of the social and political order.

The lesson, if we wish to draw a lesson, is the fragility of civilization and the resilience of culture. Once Western science and technology burst on the world, the onward march of Western civilization was probably irresistible; but that does not mean that it was destined to continue forever, or that there are no limits. In fact, it looks as though we are running up against the limits more quickly than most people expected. First, the much discussed material limits, shortages, depletion, pollution; but also the cultural limits – namely, the resistance of mankind everywhere to the levelling process of a uniform cultural pattern and the dwindling powers of assimilation of a civilization weakened by internal crisis. It is important, at the end of a study which has been concerned mainly with the rise and spread of Western civilization, to emphasize these limits. It is a necessary corrective to our preoccupation with the achievements of modern technocratic society.

The antithesis – and often the clash – between culture and civilization is one of the fundamental facts of history; and the historical record shows that in the end it is usually culture that comes out on top. It has hardier roots in human nature, acclimatized as it is over the centuries to life in small communities and to the bonds of a common experience and a common culture. The anonymous world of the great civilizations is not our natural habitat. We have other loyalties, closer, older, more insistent, and in the end more enduring. That is the fatal flaw of civilizations, the reason why they crumble and fall – not because of economic exhaustion, or because they are spread too thin and wide, but because they are rejected by the disinherited peoples within them and outside. We can see the rejection gathering force in Rome after the end of the second century of the Christian era, the growing alienation of what Toynbee called the internal and external proletariat. It would be foolish to suppose – though many people evidently still do – that our civilization is an exception to the rule. In many ways, because of its complexity, its sophistication, and its dependence upon an elaborate technological apparatus, it is more fragile and vulnerable than Rome ever was.

That does not mean, as we are often told, that we are threatened with imminent disaster. All civilizations rise and fall, but when, at what speed, and by what hidden processes, no one can foretell. No doubt there is always a possibility that a natural calamity will overtake us. A series of successive droughts would quickly turn California into desert again; an earthquake could destroy its cities and ·with them its teeming population. Such eventualities, like nuclear war, are incalculable. At the moment, all we can safely say is that we seem to have reached, perhaps passed, a turning point, that the wave of Western civilization is ebbing, not rising. It is easy, particularly for the beneficiaries, to regard this reversal as a catastrophe, and in all likelihood the years ahead, the years of adjustment to a new social environment, will be turbulent and difficult. There is even a possibility, perhaps more than a possibility, that we shall not make the adjustment. But only those who believe that modern industrial civilization represents some sort of apotheosis are likely to regret its passing; and even among its beneficiaries, they are increasingly few. What we are beginning to learn today is that cultural differences matter. Everywhere, from the Soviet Union to South-east Asia, national minorities are reasserting their autonomy, demanding decentralization and devolution, and struggling to preserve their cultural identity. Sometimes the protests are dramatic, like that of the Buddhist monks in Vietnam who set fire to themselves in protest against the assault on their culture by what they considered the false and perverted values of North American civilization. More often they take the form of mass-meetings and street-demonstrations, Georgians protesting against Russian domination, Abkhazians against Georgian. In any case, what is significant is the resilience of ancient cultures. Under their impetus, it seems, we are moving, by slow but inexorable stages, from a world of great, expanding, all-engulfing civilizations to a world of smaller, tighter, more homogeneous societies, more stable and more durable because they have their roots in history and are fortified by centuries of common experience.

If this is the outline of the world which is emerging, it will almost necessarily be a simpler, less ambitious world. The technocratic view of the future – the view that equates quantitative growth with progress – has lost its savour and its credibility. Even the underdeveloped nations of Asia, Africa and Latin America – much as they need roads, schools, electric power, machines and the rest of the apparatus of modern civilization – are beginning to realize that salvation does not lie simply in acquiring Western technology or in the vain dream of 'catching up' with the West. For them, also, the immediate task is to find an equilibrium which will enable them to attain a decent standard of living and at the same time preserve their own distinctive cultural values. For the peoples of the West the challenge is different. We enjoy, with rare exceptions, the benefits of the affluent society. Do we intend to go down with them, like the pampered, decadent Gallo-Roman senatorial families of whom we read in the pages of Gregory of Tours, unable and unwilling to adjust to changes they could not control? The problem of the West is not a lack but a surfeit of civilization. Our task today is to harness its achievements to human needs, as the great founders of modern science in the seventeenth century intended they should be harnessed. We have accumulated all we need, probably more than we need. The question now is whether we are ready to call a halt, and adapt ourselves to a simpler way of life, before we are forced to call a halt whether we want to or not. If our object is to live our three score years and ten (or perhaps, through the advance of modern medicine, three score years and sixteen or seventeen) with a sense of identity and personal dignity, a simpler life can be a fuller life. It is as easy to over-estimate as it is to under-estimate the benefits of civilization.

One of the paradoxes of the interdependent world created by the spread of Western industrial society is that interdependence makes it more, not less, important to respect and tolerate differences of culture, values and ways of living. Otherwise the prospects for peace are slender. What we have to learn is that there are stronger forces in history than the progress of science and technology. Civilization, as we understand it, is running into a dead end; culture, in the sense of the cultivation of our inherent diversities, opens a road into the future. The challenge for our generation – one of the many challenges in an age of ferment and upheaval – is to discover how to reconcile civilization and culture. It is a formidable challenge, and no other civilization has found an answer to it. But if we fail, we may be sure that culture will take a cruel revenge. The world is full of great cities which have disappeared in the sands. There is no reason why ours may not disappear likewise. I sometimes wonder whether, fifteen hundred years from now, archaeologists may not be digging in the sand-covered ruins of Los Angeles, looking for artefacts to cast light on the mores of its former inhabitants. My fear is that what they discover will be judged inferior, culturally and artistically, to Petra or Pompeii or Ch'ang-an. We are told that civilizations, even if they rise and fall, ascend a sort of spiral staircase, each successively one step ahead of the last. But if civilized life is our aim – and if it is not, what are we seeking on earth except release from earthly misery? – what has Los Angeles to offer (or any other great modern metropolis of your preference) that Ch'ang-an did not offer better? Or even Alexandria in its heyday? Those may be rhetorical questions, but it is important to think about them, for they go to the heart of the question of culture and civilization, on which – perhaps more than is often realized – the future depends.

Index